MV Hughes Glomar Explorer

~

The Top Secret Mission

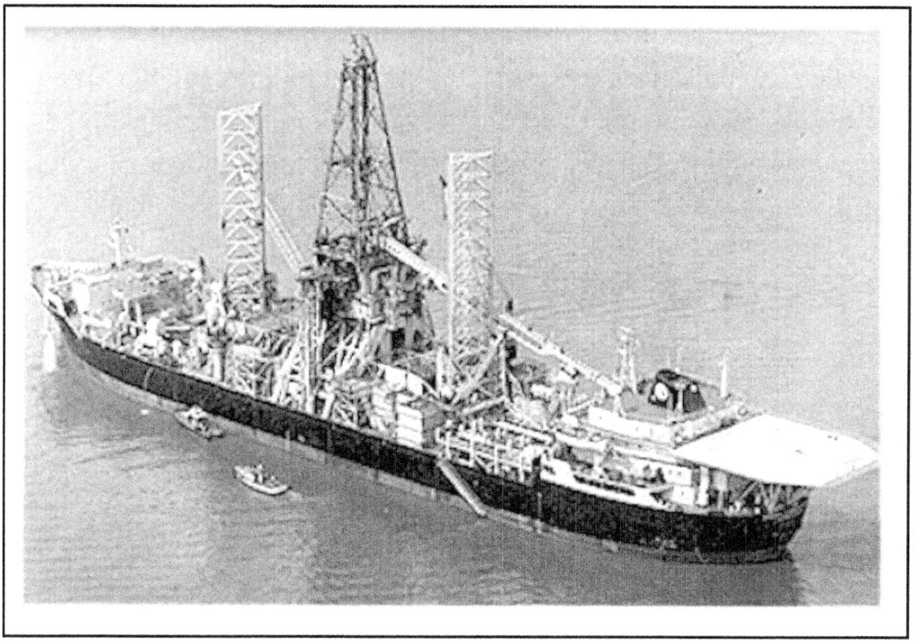

Dedication:

This book is dedicated to the engineers and managers who made this project possible.

Table Of Contents:

Project AZORIAN: 2

The Soviet Submarine: 5

Engineering For AZORIAN: 9

Early Soviet Confusion: 22

Construction and Delivery of HGE: 25

Security for Project AZORIAN: 30

The World's Largest Submersible: 57

My Darling Clementine: 63

Hanging By A Thread: 73

The Price Tag: 87

HGE Trials And Tests: 92

Mission Financing: 102

Security Operations: 115

Summa Robbery: 116

Lift-off: 130

Soviet Surveillance: 136

Recovery Completed: 138

MATADOR Preparations: 147

A Final Word: 152

Introduction:

Right after the end of World War Two, tensions between the Unites States and the Soviet Union began what is described as the Cold War era. It lasted for nearly 45 years—right up until the collapse of the Eastern Bloc in 1991. Even though during that time there were no major direct conflicts between the two super-powers, both world powers did engage in proxy wars against each other. The Berlin Blockade and the Cuban Missile Crisis are just two examples of these.

Early on the Soviet Union also began transitioning into developing a massive nuclear arsenal. Since the Unites States had already dropped atomic bombs on Hiroshima and Nagasaki, their development of nuclear weapons progressed rapidly. On the 29th of August, 1949, the Soviet Union tested their first nuclear device, and eventually they developed long-range ballistic missiles. Their submarine fleet was upgraded to use these technologies in the 1960's and on the 8th of March, 1968, they had an accident in their fleet of submarines. They lost one in the Pacific Ocean, and the United States devised a plan to try and recover her remains.

Recently the CIA released documents on this Top Secret mission, and how one ship was built to carry out this program. She was named the Glomar Explorer (with her official title being the MV Hughes Glomar Explorer). By chance I had seen her during my time while attending the California Maritime Academy, since I would occasionally drive over the nearby Martinez Bridge—while passing by Suisun Bay—where I could see the Mothball Fleet at anchor. Most of the ships were from the World War II era, all resting peacefully in a large grouping awaiting a call up that would never happen. But there was one ship that stood out amongst them and was quickly spotted. The Hughes Glomar Explorer was easy to notice as she was much larger than the others and had an unusual design. She also carried with her the secrets of an important project. At that time it was still mostly rumors, as little had been documented other than what was reported in the newspapers. But now much more is known, and this is meant to give her story, from two different perspectives—from that of the Soviet Union, and from that of the United States. *The Soviet side is printed in italics to show the distinction between the two.*

Project AZORIAN:

In March of 1968 a Soviet submarine of the G-II class was lost with all hands, 16,500 feet below the surface of the Pacific Ocean.

On the 8th of August, 1974, portions of that submarine were brought to the surface by using a recovery system designed and developed specifically for that mission.

The story of the more than six years intervening is the story of Project AZORIAN, that is, the story of the MV Hughes Glomar Explorer.

AZORIAN ranks in the forefront of imaginative and bold operations undertaken in the long history of intelligence collection. It combined immense size and scope, advanced developments with technology, complex systems engineering and testing, extremely severe cover and security requirements, a demanding mission scenario in an unforgiving marine environment, the potential for a serious confrontation with the Soviet Union, a difficult exploitation phase, and high cost.

The project eventually became widely known to the media in early 1975. At a time when the Central Intelligence Agency (CIA) was under investigation by two different committees of Congress and many members of the press, they were credited in some newspaper editorials with pursuing their tradecraft in a most imaginative manner and doing what intelligence organizations are supposed to do—collect intelligence. Still other articles were critical of the project, its cost, and its method of operation.

Many senior U.S. Government officials, including three Directors of Central Intelligence, two Secretaries of Defense, two Secretaries of State, and two Presidents, were personally knowledgeable of the program and recognized it as an innovative undertaking of great magnitude and complexity. Key members of four Congressional committees were also kept informed of the project's progress and reviewed budget requests for AZORIAN.

Due to the AZORIAN project having such huge dimensions in cost, risk, and intelligence value, it sometimes caused difficult problems for the officials who had to make the major decisions affecting it. Some of the questions didn't lend themselves to clear-cut unequivocal answers: the intelligence value of the target after six years on the ocean floor, for example, or the political or physical response of the Russians if they should learn of the recovery effort.

Because of these difficult questions, there couldn't be and wasn't unanimity of opinion among senior officials in the departments at CIA, Defense, State, the White House, and other agencies collectively responsible for AZORIAN and the decision on whether or not to proceed.

Differences of opinion were expressed and debated in the appropriate forums, both before the project was initiated and during its lifetime. These differences are expressed candidly in several places.

In March of 1975 columnist Jack Anderson disclosed the existence of the MV Hughes Glomar Explorer (HGE) project on national television and radio. The original press leak had occurred in the Los Angeles Times in February of 1975. The Times story was unspecific and wrong in important facts, but it gradually developed into a widespread security problem for the program even before the Anderson disclosure had happened.

The original leak resulted from an improbable series of events following a break-in and robbery in June of 1974 at Summa Corporation headquarters in Los Angeles. It was thought that amongst the stolen documents there might be a memorandum from a senior Hughes official to Howard Hughes describing a proposed CIA attempt to recover a sunken Soviet submarine and requesting Hughes' approval for Hughes Company to participate.

Thus it became necessary to brief several persons involved in the investigation in order to protect the document from disclosure—if it were recovered. While the source of the leak was never identified, the circumstances became known to the reporters who were covering the story and it ended up disclosed in the Los Angeles Times story.

Extraordinary efforts being led by the Director of Central Intelligence (DCI) Colby and others would contain the spread of the story for a time, but it eventually became widely known within press circles, and Anderson decided to break it.

Project Origins:

The diesel-powered K-129 Soviet G-II-class ballistic missile submarine pendant 722 sailed from Petropavlovsk in late February of 1968 to take a patrol station northeast of Hawaii, off the west coast of the United States, where she would be available for a nuclear attack on U.S. targets in the event of a war. (Figure 1.) The submarine suffered an accident—cause unknown—and sank 1,560 miles northwest of Hawaii. With the K-129 out of contact and overdue, the Soviets undertook a massive two-month search effort covering a broad area from Petropavlovsk to the patrol area northeast of Hawaii. However, the Soviet search was fruitless.

Senior officials in the Department of Defense and CIA recognized that if it were feasible to devise a plan to recover important components of the submarine, extremely valuable information on Soviet strategic capabilities could be obtained.

Figure 1. The K-129 submarine showing hull number 722.

The Soviet Submarine:

K-129 had already completed combat patrols in late 1967, and the veteran crew had gone home on leave. This would normally have been down time in port for the submarine (for maintenance, training and personnel vacation time), but something happened—a different submarine scheduled to leave on the next patrol wasn't prepared, and then a second submarine also failed their inspection, so the departed K-129 crew was called back again in early 1968 by headquarters to report for sea. And they were informed it was imperative that as a replacement they get out quickly, since Brezhnev was rattling tails and *we couldn't let the Americans know the fleet was having issues (Our country must strive for naval supremacy and these diesel submarines were an important part of that program, at any cost.) Never mind the remoteness of the area—with the nuclear fleet just really becoming established—and all the difficulties with the maintenance and crewing involved in such a forbidding place. Just hurry and get out to sea!*

The entire crew needed for the mission would total close to 100 personnel, but out of this—due to the rush nature of the voyage—they would have 25 new crew members coming aboard, with 10 of those requiring on the job training. So it would be up to the 58 returning veteran members to make up for them, and they would have to do it all in short order—since some had arrived barely a few days prior to departure (and since they were put together so hurriedly—someone had even forgotten to keep an official crew list at the command post).

To accomplish this mission, headquarters trusted Captain First Rank Cobzar to keep things aboard the boat running smoothly, after all—he already had four years sailing aboard this same submarine, and had lengthy sub experience from within the rest of the fleet. He went along with the plan as a good submariner, even though privately some were questioning the rational for sending them out on such short notice like this.

So on the bitterly cold morning of February 24th in 1968, off the east coast of the Soviet Union—the Kamchatka peninsula to be exact—by a city once named by Bering after a couple of his own ships—K-129 left the dock to head out, on a mission scheduled to last until the 5th of May (for a total voyage length of 70 days), out for scheduled patrol duty in the Northeast Pacific Ocean.

Soviet operation orders were to regularly inform Pacific Fleet Headquarters at certain intervals while underway, which was done shortly after they tested the submarine on a first dive. The reply was sent back and all seemed well.

The next scheduled message was for the 12th of March (passing the 180th meridian), but as time passed by, nothing was received for a communications check. The submarine was still days away from being in the combat patrol area, so headquarters dismissed it as just an anomaly.

However, when news broke about the U.S. submarine Swordfish having arrived in Japan with damages on the 18th of that month, it aroused suspicions of a possible collision with K-129 (the U.S. Navy would have attack submarines tailing the Soviet subs after they'd left our port). Add to that another scheduled communications check with headquarters was missed, and it was obvious that something went wrong aboard K-129, and we needed to find out what.

Hastily a search effort was put together based on the submarine's cruising speed of 12 knots, concentrating on the northwest portion of the Pacific Ocean, using aircraft to search the ocean surface, and having ships use sonar to listen for any signals. Everyone initially hoped to find that the submarine was on the surface in distress, simply unable to send messages. But as the days passed by, things shifted to the worst case scenario—assuming a total loss—and for search efforts to now look for any signs of debris or sounds that might help to locate the missing sub and her crew.

Meanwhile, U.S. Intelligence was also interested in where the submarine had ended up, as they were monitoring the progress of the search area as well. Since the U.S. Navy had a sound surveillance system (SOSUS) deployed in the Pacific, it was used to try and determine if it had any data on a possible location. After checking, they found that several arrays had recorded a large noise that triangulated to an area hundreds of miles away from where the Soviet main search was happening. The U.S. data narrowed the location down to within a 5 nautical mile area for the accident site, and this knowledge was kept a secret for now.

Eventually our Soviet military finished the search area covering over a million miles, ultimately using destroyers, patrol ships, auxiliary vessels, submarines, and aircraft, but nothing was found other than unrelated oil slicks and normal ocean debris. So things slowly went back to normal and the search was wound down—K-129 became written off as lost at sea. Fortunately for them, the U.S. Navy had a special ship, the USNS Mizar, which had earlier been converted for underwater search in 1963, and had participated in important searches up to this point—including the loss of the USS Thresher. Her mission now was to search the sea bottom for K-129 and then assess with accuracy the state of the submarine. Such a search involved running grids back and forth over the search area, and inspecting any anomalies that were found amongst the data. For a few months this search went on, and while they found some interesting targets, none were the right one.

Then by a miracle the K-129 sub was found, and nearly intact. They placed sonar buoys to mark the area, and photographed everything carefully, then left the area. Later in August the USS Halibut arrived at the site, being an attack submarine converted to underwater special operations. She carefully surveyed the site, and this information is what led to Project AZORIAN.

While the U.S. Navy now knew the location and condition of the submarine, they pondered if it would be possible to raise her—or somehow recover the important pieces of equipment and information that they were most interested in. They found that K-129 was down at the bottom at a great depth of over 16,000 feet (3 miles). Such a depth is hard to imagine, especially when you add in the pressures involved with the ocean water itself. And assuming it could even be accomplished, how would our country react?

Engineering For AZORIAN:

The engineering aspects with the AZORIAN program were a challenge which many thought rivaled that of the space program. It was said that we know more about the backside of the moon than the bottom of the ocean. Now the CIA engineers and management were being asked to undertake in an unstudied abyss an engineering marvel—and in one gigantic effort, pull an estimated 3,920,000 pounds of wrecked submarine out of the ocean bottom and lift her intact over three miles into a surface ship. Never had such a feat before been accomplished.

The CIA was being tasked to do it not only in this poorly understood environment, but also within record time. And no one was to know about it. However, if the United States could get its hands on the Soviet subs code books and machines, the nuclear weapons, the strategic plans, and ... well, it was just too plain good to be true. Their potential value was inestimable. To have it all tomorrow would hardly be soon enough. These were the pressures the CIA felt, especially the line managers and the engineers.

There is no way to describe the engineering for Project AZORIAN without bringing in the facts and figures, for to ignore them would leave a gaping hole in the AZORIAN story. Because it was these very facts and figures—so fascinating to the engineer and so fearsome to the layman—that must prove the project's feasibility. They along with the engineers who made them a reality were essential to becoming the true underpinnings of Project AZORIAN.

Organizing for Recovery:

Discussions regarding the feasibility of recovering components of K-129 took place between technical representatives of the CIA and the Department of Defense during the latter months of 1968 and into early 1969. These talks resulted in a letter to the Director of Central Intelligence, Richard Helms, from the Deputy Secretary of Defense, David Packard, on the 1st of April, 1969. Packard, referring to the sunken submarine, asked for a study of what could be done in the next few years to recover the significant components. He asked the CIA to take the lead and designated Dr. John Foster, Director of Defense Research and Engineering (DD/R&E) as the point for coordination. Mr. Helms designated Carl Duckett, Deputy Director for Science and Technology (DD/S&T) as the CIA focal point.

During early July in 1969 the CIA representatives, including John Parangosky and others, worked to develop a plan for a program to recover the submarine. This plan was coordinated and approved by mid-July in 1969.

On the 17th of July, 1969, Helms advised Packard that considerable work had already been accomplished to undertake the submarine's recovery; that Duckett had met with and work was in progress to develop a charter for it, and that an Agency task force was studying the retrieval problems associated with the sunken G-II submarine.

On the 8th of August, 1969, it was outlined to a high-level Executive Committee (ExCom consisted of Packard as Chairman; with Helms; and the Science Advisor to the President, Dr. Lee DuBridge) the proposed organization for the submarine recovery effort, including structure, management, assets, personnel assignments, and intelligence objectives.

ExCom approved the establishment of the new organization and the allocation of resources and personnel, and agreed that the President should be advised of its establishment. This was done in a memorandum from Dr. Kissinger to President Nixon, which the President approved of.

An agreement describing the organization's detailed responsibilities, management structure, and working relationships was signed on the 19th of August, 1969. Among other features, it specified that the staffing of the new organization should reflect the best talent available from the CIA. Security policy and procedures were in accordance with the basic agreement, which placed security management responsibility for the new security system, code-named JENNIFER, with the Director of Security, CIA, acting for the DCI.

From the beginning, extraordinary security was imposed and clearances severely limited to those with an absolute need-to-know. It was clear at all stages of the AZORIAN Project that it had to be leak-proof to enable the mission to be conducted without diplomatic or physical interference from the Soviets. Therefore, air-tight security and effective cover were of the utmost importance, and the projects continuation depended upon them completely.

Security For Project AZORIAN:

The technological feats accomplished in building and operating the MV Hughes Glomar Explorer and maintaining the Hughes deep-ocean mining cover were the "up front" elements of Project AZORIAN. But behind the scenes, equally important activities also started taking place, quietly and professionally.

One of the staunchest, most dedicated groups participating in AZORIAN was the CIA's Office of Security. Their policies and their procedures provided the day-to-day shield which protected the program and the myriad of people working on it. It was the individual security officers assigned to the program who implemented the policies and procedures, or often quickly improvised new ones on the spot for unusual situations. They provided the rivets that held the security shield together and in place.

The immediate purpose of the security shield was to prevent the leakage of information to the news media. Its ultimate purpose, of course, was the denial to the Soviets of any shred of knowledge about the true objectives of the program.

The first security officer on the scene set the tone and standards for security from Day One. He was followed by more than 20 others who were assigned for varying lengths of time directly to the AZORIAN project, and its related activities. They were supported by the unheralded troops in the Office of Security's field offices and in the trenches at Headquarters who did the routine legwork and desk-work so essential to the maintenance of a successful security program.

The dedication and hard work of all the officers made it possible for the program to run as long as it did without the erosion of the cover story and without a breakdown in program security.

Establishing the Security Base:

The CIA-Department of Defense agreement which established AZORIAN as a priority program was signed on the 19th of August, 1969. It gave the security management responsibility to the Director of Security, CIA, who would act for the Director of Central Intelligence. The Director of Security had already asked the chief of his Special Security Center to assume day-to-day responsibility for the compartmentalization which would be necessary to protect program information.

The first security officer had been assigned to the embryonic Special Projects Staff and had been drawing up the over-all security plan, as well as the specifics for the AZORIAN program.

It was the security plan that was code-named JENNIFER, and because this word would appear on the cover of all AZORIAN-related documents, among those on the fringes of the program—it also became synonymous with the project itself.

By the 15th of July, 1969, a draft of the security plan was sent to the DOD for comment and on the day the AZORIAN project agreement was signed, the first JENNIFER security guide was issued. This policy paper was a 13-page directive covering the background of the program, the general security policy, all personnel security, personnel restrictions and requirements, any physical security, contracting and funding security, necessary communications security and public information control.

The second security directive was issued on the 12th of December, 1969, and spelled out procedures for handling program documents within government and industry. Industrial aspects of security were to grow increasingly important as the commercial nature of the AZORIAN cover plan unfolded.

The program manager had a philosophy about security that proved to be invaluable; it was especially applicable to the movement into a new world of commercial cover and security for a major technical effort. This philosophy was that security would be involved in every aspect of the program, including planning, from the very first day of operations.

Security wasn't to be used just to clean up a mess or tamp down flaps after they'd developed. It was to be a part of all program deliberations. The approval of security was to be obtained before any action was taken. In this way many potential problems were avoided or finessed without causing a stir. The security officers responded to the philosophy with an attitude of "How can we help you solve your problem?" In this way a healthy and mutual respect developed between the engineers with their enormous engineering problems and the security officers who were charged with protecting this "Mission Impossible" from disclosure.

Development of Engineering Concept:

The original CIA task force for Project AZORIAN was established on the 1st of July, 1969, and became the program headquarters complement, while John Parangosky, who had previously held key assignments within the Agency, was named to head this staff. Parangosky initially assembled a small task force of engineers and technicians, who were closeted each day in a large room dubbed the "think tank," to develop an engineering concept to recover the Soviet submarine.

Because of the great difficulty and complexity of the recovery problem, the task force called on three security-cleared contractors for early help concerning structures and mechanisms, naval architecture, and also for sensors. Principal criteria for the recovery concept were technical and operational feasibility, timeliness of implementation (get the system out into the field as soon as possible for an early recovery mission), and reasonableness of costs. The group quickly immersed itself into the problem, fully aware of the challenges of this uniquely difficult task. They knew that no country in the world had ever succeeded in raising an object of this size and weight from such a depth before.

Early Concepts:

Three basic categories of lift concepts were considered for use in these early studies: the total "brute force" or direct lift; a trade ballast/buoyancy; and an at-depth generation of buoyancy. Each is reviewed below:

a. Total "Brute Force" (Direct) Lift, referred to as the Rosenberg Winch, would involve massive floating winches with wire ropes of the necessary strength to manage the total weight of the target object (believed at that time to be about 2,000 to 2,200 long tons).

Use of a "drill string" (i.e., a "string" of connecting pipe) was discarded by the task force in the early discussions because it was difficult to calculate how the required massive pipe could be successfully deployed. It was believed at that time that the weight of the pipe alone couldn't be supported from the surface and still allow enough strength and lifting capacity on the submarine hull section.

b. In the Trade Ballast/ Buoyancy concept, a buoyant material would be carried to the bottom using an excess of ballast. Then once at the bottom, the excess ballast would be dropped away, generating sufficient positive buoyancy to extricate the target from the bottom and help to lift it to the surface.

c. An At-Depth Generation of Buoyancy concept used the generation of enough gas at depth to create sufficient buoyancy to lift the target. Various methods reviewed included using the electrolysis of sea water, cryogenic gases (hydrogen, nitrogen), catalytic decomposition of hydrazine, and chemical generation of hydrogen through the reaction of active metals (e.g., sodium, lithium) or metal hydrides (e.g., lithium hydride).

Feasibility Studies:

Because the target was judged to be of a great value to the intelligence community, the higher echelons of the U.S. Government had decided it was a "go" situation before the technical feasibility studies were even completed. Those were the days in which it was assumed American technology could eventually solve any problem.

Impinging on the feasibility studies was the fact that the recovery system was to be used in a one-time effort. There was no way in which a full-scale test could be run within the available time, fiscal, and design constraints. To design, build, and test the recovery and lift equipment for multiple use would have increased the costs to an unacceptable level.

AZORIAN therefore would have to be a single-shot, go-for-broke effort.

To turn a "go" situation into a "go" decision for the U.S. Government, three fundamental questions needed to be answered. One of the answers was provided early in 1970 by the drilling ship Glomar Challenger, operated by Global Marine Inc. for the National Science Foundation. The question was, "Can a large surface ship maintain a position accurately enough at sea in order to lower a string of pipe to an exact geographic position on the ocean bottom?" The answer became a resounding "yes." The Challenger rig had drilled a hole in the deep ocean floor, withdrawn the drill bit, and then successfully re-entered the hole. This feat required maintaining the surface ship to within a circle whose radius was on the order of only 15 feet, a major success by any measure.

Engineering Concept Selected:

The other two questions involved the heavy lift portion of the recovery system, in particular the heavy lift pipe. One question concerned the ability to make pieces of pipe of the requisite strength and quality in large enough numbers. The other concerned the effects on the ship and her drilling platform if the pipe string should break while under a maximum load. This could transform a controlled, 17-million-pound, relatively static load into an uncontrolled dynamic one. Or, as the Deputy Director, Research and Engineering for the Department of Defense (a nuclear physicist) stated when first advised of the magnitude of the effect, "That's the energy equivalent of setting off a nuclear explosive of 8 kilotons." Needless to say, such an analogy didn't lessen any concerns with management. And while the satisfactory answers to these questions and others weren't available in the early days—they were arrived at later. But the lack of answers at this time didn't stall the program, thanks to an important decision made by management.

By late July in 1970, the heavy-lift concept became clearly the favored system to develop for the recovery mission. And from this time on, it was given the full attention by all the appropriate parties, until the formal authorization to concentrate all studies on the heavy-lift method was officially given on the 11th of September in 1970, during a briefing at the Pentagon.

And as this engineering concept was being formalized, a deep-ocean mining cover story was also beginning to take form to explain all the project's activities, particularly those planned for the various at-sea operations to come.

Executive Committee Approval:

At the 30th of October, 1970, Executive Committee (ExCom) meeting, the matter of conceptual development for the target recovery was addressed. It described the dead-lift (or brute force) concept which would be designed to lift the estimated 1,750-ton target object from the 16,500-foot depth by means of using heavy-lifting equipment mounted on a large (565' by 106') surface ship.

As previously mentioned, a deep-sea mining venture was to be used as the cover story for this operation. To support this theory, a mining device would be constructed which could be handled by the surface ship and mated into her center well. A submersible dry dock was also planned to complete the system.

As with all engineering concepts, many technical risk areas were involved, and so they tried identifying the major ones. These were characterized as being within the state-of-the-art design but required a major beef-up to handle the weights and pressures involved. The control system was also considered a risk area, but its feasibility had already been demonstrated by another Global Marine ship, the Glomar

Challenger, which had drilled a hole in the sea floor and withdrawn the drill bit—then placed a new bit into the same drill hole in deep water earlier in 1970. It was further pointed out that an extensive simulation program would also be conducted to define the dynamic characteristics and stresses of the system. However so far an initial analysis hadn't uncovered any unexpected or insurmountable problems.

All in all, even at this time it was estimated that the probability of success was only about 10 percent— not a very reassuring number. (However, this estimate continued to rise as the design, development, and testing proceedings moved along. Just prior to the mission, it was believed the probability of success had risen to be nearly 90 percent.) Also, Helms stated that the ad hoc committee of the U.S. Intelligence Board (USIB) had completed a detailed review of the value of the AZORIAN target on which they had placed the highest priority, and he concurred in their assessment.

Others pointed out at the meeting that there were two basic questions to be answered: should the organization proceed all-out with AZORIAN? If so, where would the necessary funding be obtained? Packard answered that not all data on fund availability was known yet, but that they nevertheless should go ahead with the AZORIAN project.

Some concluding remarks were made by others at the meeting. Dr. John Foster, Director of Defense Research & Engineering, observed that there appeared to be an underestimation by those present on the value of the target. Helms commented that he was more confident in regards to this project than to some others because of the thorough work that had been done up to this point. Packard summed up the proceedings of this meeting and said the consensus was to proceed with AZORIAN. He felt that planning should continue but said it would be necessary to identify possible sources of funding.

An Important Decision:

The project managers also made a key decision in the fall of 1970 that the design and construction of the hardware would proceed on a concurrent basis. Several factors led to this decision. There were perishable aspects to the program including the cryptographic material being sought, as well as the cover and the security. The yearly two-month weather window for the operation also became a factor. A delay of two months in the design and construction would mean a 12-month slip in the operation length. A delay of this magnitude would add maintenance costs to the program and magnify the chances for cover and security erosion. Therefore nothing was simple; all factors were inextricably tied together. With the knowledge available at the time, the only prudent decision was to go ahead on a concurrent basis. To wait until all the technical risks were resolved would mean not only more dollars spent, but perhaps no mission at all.

In October of 1970 the engineering staff faced 11 major unknowns or technical risk areas. Problems existed in all elements of the program and included such basic items as the exact dimensions and the condition of the target, the recovery ship design, the working machinery to provide the lift capability, the pipe string, etc. Therefore, the unknowns and their individual solutions presented a frightening array of interfaces still needing to be resolved.

Four to eight months for each of the 11 unknowns was estimated as necessary to get better definitions; that totaled 60 months in all. If the engineers had to wait for a sequential resolution for each of the risk areas, at least three to four years would be added to the schedule. Furthermore, the entanglement of each of the items with all the rest meant that a solution to one would affect all of the others. And no final solution could be obtained until all of them were resolved. So the only way to handle this situation was to start the design and construction on a concurrent basis, recognizing that changes would have to be made and that the designs would have to be kept flexible to accommodate them. In fact, senior management at the national level recognized that in some cases they might have to build the hardware in order to resolve the problems; since design alone wouldn't be able to do it. This proved to be prescience of the first order with regard to the pipe handling system, and even with the design of the ship.

The concurrent design/construction philosophy that kept flexibility in the program paid off handsomely in an area that wasn't fully anticipated in the fall of 1970. To fit the target inside the ship required that the well be widened, which in turn added 10 feet to the beam (the width) of the ship. And while this caused a dollar increase in the program—the other alternative would have been more costly. In this aspect alone, program costs would have become greater than those under the concurrent design/construction philosophy because of the additional year of program activity.

It's easy to see that it took a high order of vision and courage for the program managers and engineers to go with the concurrent design/construction philosophy. They recognized that it would mean changes and cost increases from the baseline given in October of 1970, and that they could incur ex post facto criticism of their decision. But they made this decision and stuck to it, and it proved to be vital to the program. Without it, the project might have died during birth or incurred costs far in excess of what they eventually turned out to be.

Engineering Organization:

The interwoven and potentially chaotic engineering responsibilities for the design and construction were managed by a four-level planning structure. (see Figure 2.)

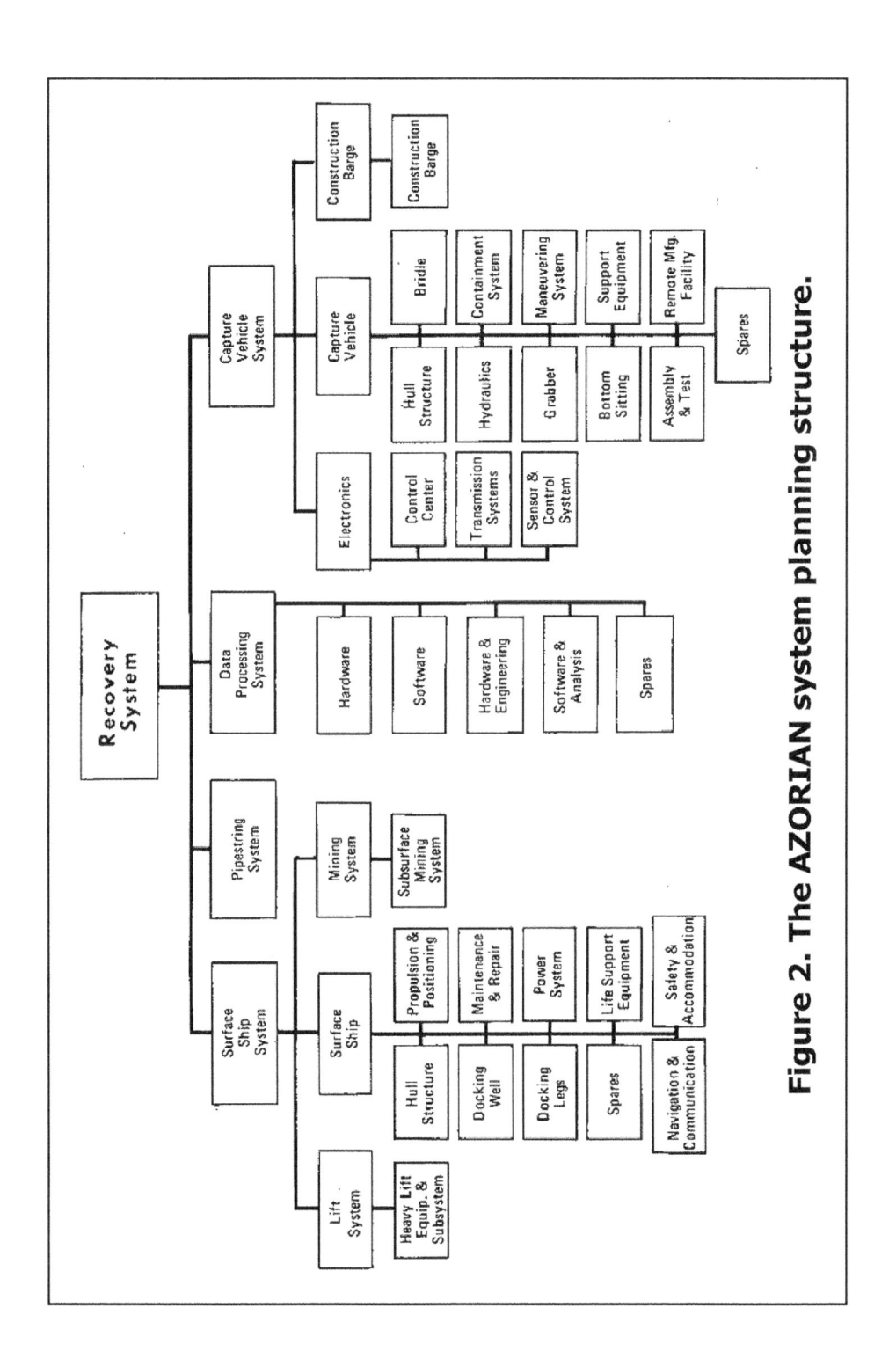

Figure 2. The AZORIAN system planning structure.

The highest level (0) was the over-all recovery system, the totality of the hardware. The next level (1) contained the four principal hardware systems and contractors, which were the surface ship system (Global Marine), the pipe string system (Summa/Hughes Tool Co.), the capture vehicle system, and the data processing system (Honeywell). These were broken down into their major components for the next lower level (2). Finally the lowest level (3)—to be controlled by CIA project engineers—contained the major components of Level 2. Obviously, the levels could go on ad infinitum, but it was concluded that major decisions wouldn't go below Level 3; therefore, the lower levels were supervised by contractor engineers under the direction of Agency engineers.

Project AZORIAN was managed by the Special Projects Staff (SPS) of the CIA's Directorate of Science & Technology. Within SPS the engineering group was headed by a single individual while his staff comprised only seven additional engineers, which was an incredibly small number to manage this complex and costly system. Needless to say, each of them was "a rambling wreck and a helluva engineer."

Early Soviet Confusion:

*W*hy was the main search area so far off from where the submarine had actually sunk? Did the Captain decide to go rogue, and go off away from orders? K-129 had apparently traveled south from Kamchatka until reaching the 40th parallel of latitude (for radio communications security reasons), and then went due east from there, finally sinking at the 180th meridian. How strange. No communications though, even though they must've been able to transmit on the scheduled day. Rumors went around, and even some of the wives found out back then and asked questions. But all they heard for an answer was just wait, they'll come back.

Normally international law makes warships immune from recovery by foreign governments, so our government might have called this an act of piracy. It could've created an international incident, and was a risk not only to the U.S., but to the recovery team conducting such a mission. With regular merchant vessels lost it could be called a simple salvage operation—all perfectly legal—but not with this one.

On the other hand, the Soviet brass had picked out a poor area to search, ensuring it wouldn't be found by us. And in the Stalinist manner, we took what comes and regarded the loss as a sacrifice for the mother country. The family members of the lost crew were left not knowing why they were gone, or even where. After too many months of slow-walking the issue, eventually the death certificates would arrive that only stated "Declared Dead" and little else. Nothing was reported in the Soviet press mentioning the crew either, they were lost and the government wanted them forgotten.

And why would the United States even bother to find such a submarine after all? It was older technology at that point, and the key encrypted codes were already changed after her loss. Just to find the submarine would be a miracle, and then what could they do with it? There was no technology at the time to raise her, much less take everything back and keep it. There was nothing to worry about, said the Soviet brass. "We haven't found our sub, and neither can they."

On paper it probably seemed all plausible, as there was no technology to raise the sub. She was about 100 meters long after all (330 feet) with a beam of 28 feet. But we were forgetting, only a few years earlier the first man had began circling the Earth in a spacecraft, and that might never have seemed possible either. Could such a sub be raised to the surface? Only time would tell—but it wouldn't be done by us.

Maybe there was more to this submarine than was being passed off here. During 1966—1967 the K-129 had been upgraded to a newer weapons system, and had passed all of her repair trials. It was now officially classified as a 629A by the Soviet Navy, meaning she had a newer missile system capable of carrying three R-21 missiles that could be launched from inside their tubes while still submerged, while having a longer range to target. But it was still a diesel, and needed to charge her storage batteries out at sea. This meant snorkeling in the winter sea, a dangerous procedure at any time. While using a snorkel mast and just being under the surface, a vigilant watch was needed to make sure nothing was hit, or nothing flooded. And worst of all, outside sounds couldn't be heard on sonar itself due to the loud diesel engines being run constantly.

This could've been when the accident started. A float valve froze or got flooded, maybe the mast wasn't closed properly. It was imperative that they not surface as in the old days during pre-radar.

Or it was surmised that the USS Swordfish had actually struck K-129 as she altered course onto a new heading, while being tailed and moving side to side. At the exact wrong time—a course change came, while the Swordfish was on that side of the sub. A strike to the underneath might have occurred, accounting for the damage to the sail area on the Swordfish when she arrived in port. Officially, the U.S. Navy claimed it was a bent periscope damaged from pack ice while surfacing around the Sea of Japan. But if K-129 sank on the 8th of March, and the Swordfish arrived in Japan on the 17th, that meant nine days were used to travel 2000 nautical miles (certainly possible considering the cruising speed of that submarine), while a trip straight to Hawaii would've looked even worse.

Recovery Systems Modification:

It was reported back to ExCom on the 24th of March, 1971, on the technical and design progress of AZORIAN. Total cost now was projected to rise with the principal cost increases attributable to two factors: (1) the necessary extended operations to permit a more adequate systems testing, and (2) cover enhancement and recomputation of all general and administrative expenses. Increases in hardware costs were relatively small.

Construction and Delivery of HGE:

In April of 1971, Robert F. Bauer, chairman of the board of Global Marine, Inc., had issued a press release announcing that they would begin building a 600-foot mining ship for the Hughes Tool Company (HTC). The following month, the GMI Quarterly Financial Report to the stockholders mentioned that a preliminary agreement had been reached with Sun Shipbuilding Company for the construction of the ship. On the 4th of November, 1972, the MV Hughes Glomar Explorer was launched with the usual champagne christening ceremony and speeches by Bauer and Paul Reeve, general manager of the Ocean Mining Division of the HTC. At the same time, a press release was made available to the news media providing general information about the MV Hughes Glomar Explorer and some of the principal contractors involved in her construction.

The Surface Ship:

The MV Hughes Glomar Explorer, or as she came to be known, the HGE, was created from a vision in one man's mind. John Graham of Global Marine was the chief designer and supervisor of construction. It was the culmination of his career as a naval architect. For anyone who had anything to do with the design and construction of the HGE, John was the hub around which all the engineering activity took place. A man who was often deep into the details, he was nevertheless single-minded in his efforts to construct a ship that would do a salvage job heretofore believed impossible.

HGE Requirements:

Simply stated, the requirement for the surface ship system was to pick up 3,920,000 pounds (1750 tons or the equivalent of a World War II light destroyer) from the ocean floor, then lift it over 3 miles to the surface and place it within the bowels of the recovery ship HGE. All this was to be done covertly, and allow for her crew to fulfill this mission while staying up to 100 days at sea for its completion.

These general requirements were translated into more detailed lists of very specific design requirements for each of the lower system levels. To get a flavor for what these requirements were like, two examples are presented here:

Ship Underway

Sea State	Extreme storm conditions
Wind Velocity	100 knots
Temperature	40-105°F
Pitch	15°
Roll	60°

Static Hold (Fail/Safe While Lifting Target)

Sea State	12 foot sea, 18 foot swell
Wind Velocity	50 knots
Temperature	40-105°F
Pitch	15°
Roll	22°
Heave	32 Feet
Drill Floor	
Gimbal Pitch	10°
Gimbal Roll	17°

Heave Compensator 14 Feet Working
Dead Load   17,750,000 Lbs.
Live Load   19,750,000 Lbs.
Overload (Max.)   29,800,000 Lbs.

Lists similar to these two examples were compiled for each of the sub-systems which, in total, comprised the surface ship system. Besides being interwoven amongst themselves, these requirements were also tied into all the other requirements of the other Level 1 systems.

Construction of the HGE:

During the spring of 1970 contractors were being selected to design and build the major elements of the HGE. Global Marine, because of its experience as a ship designer and fleet operator in offshore and deep ocean activities, was selected to design and build the HGE with a subcontract to Sun Shipbuilding and Drydock Co.

An initial visual assessment of the Sun Shipyard in Chester, Pa., was made from a Metroliner as it rumbled close by enroute to Philadelphia. The lift system was done by Global Marine with a subcontract to Western Gear. Global Marine also became the total system's integrator. The success of the Glomar Challenger was another factor favoring the selection of Global Marine, since they'd designed, built and operated that ship earlier for the National Science Foundation. She had an outstanding record of service and had been a huge scientific success.

By mid-1970, with the heavy lift systems concept defined, a total system design was initiated. The concurrent design/construction philosophy required continual compatibility assurance among all the elements, including extremely accurate initial design weight estimates. Rigid weight budgets were placed on the massive machinery of the lift system. Equipment was being sized relative to the estimated weights of the target, the capture vehicle, and the 16,700 feet of required drill pipe. Any erroneous estimate resulting in a major hardware overweight could stall the lift system, which wouldn't be tested under a full load until the actual mission. As it was, and in spite of some increases and some decreases, the system element weight estimates proved to be accurate in terms of the total lift. The estimated weight of the target proved conservative.

Although system designing continued into late 1971 with the publication of the major element specifications, a few long lead-time items were ordered starting in November of 1970. Major long lead-time procurement actually began in March of 1971. This included materials (steel) for the ship's hull, center well, A-frame, gimbal platforms, gimbal bearings, and the 5-foot-diameter by 20-foot-long heave compensation and heavy lift system cylinders. These latter items required from 15 to 18 months lead time and were needed for installation during the fall of 1972.

One problem which occurred in the procurement cycle was the "Buy American" policy. While many small items were available from multiple sources, two major procurements were a more severe problem and required the appropriate permission to buy foreign. Adding spice to the latter case was the delivery of the cylinders by a Communist bloc freighter.

The major elements of the system were already undergoing bid evaluation and vendor selection during late 1970 and into early 1971. By July of 1971 an improvement in the target object definition led to some major specification changes. Measurement of the effective horizontal distance from the keel to the top of the sail of the target was increased by several feet. This required widening the center well of the ship from its 69-foot width to 74 feet. This, for geometric, structural and stability reasons, increased the beam from 106 to 116 feet (now making passage through the Panama Canal impossible). The ship's length was also increased to 589'-7" at waterline or 618'-8" overall. These dimensional changes were driven as much by stability requirements as by geometric and structural considerations. Without them, the ship's self-righting capability when she rolled in heavy seas under worst-case loading conditions would be marginal. Worst-case loading would occur at the beginning of target recovery after the target had been freed from the bottom, with the combined total load estimated at 16,300,000 lbs. hanging off the gimbal platform 100 feet above the waterline. Anti-roll tanks also were incorporated into the ship's design to further improve stability in heavy seas.

Security Design and Development:

As the program moved out of this formative stage and into design with development, there was an increased demand for security approvals on contractor employees. A concerted effort was made to restrict the number of individuals briefed on AZORIAN in order to limit the targeting and penetration opportunities available to industrial and foreign espionage. But the program couldn't be done in a vacuum; contractors had to have access to the program.

Because it was an ostensibly commercial effort, all industrial personnel had to be investigated by the Office of Security without showing government interest. To have shown a U.S. Government footprint during a background investigation would have blown the cover. All personnel approved for access met the strict security criteria for AZORIAN. It was the largest effort of this type ever undertaken by the Office of Security.

Within the security approval for the program, three levels of access were established based on the need-to-know principle. The highest level gave full program knowledge and was limited to those who needed the information to carry out their part of the program and to those going on the mission.

The more remote one's activity or involvement in the program, the lower his access approval.

Mechanisms were developed to obtain other special security approvals. Certain commercially employed individuals needed access but it had to be granted without widespread knowledge within their organization. It wouldn't make sense to be granting this to all Global Marine or Hughes Tool employees. The Office of Security worked out an arrangement with their counterparts to have these clearances granted and at the same time limit the knowledge of it to only a handful of AZORIAN-cleared people. It was the use of this kind of procedure that allowed AZORIAN to move ahead on a very rapid time scale.

Security for Project AZORIAN:

During this stage of the program another landmark security decision was made. This was the so-called "team spirit approach." Contractor personnel at the top level were to be considered full members of the team. What the government knew, they would know within the area relevant to contractors. And aboard ship there were to be no second-class citizens. This policy was also maintained, while only certain information was withheld from top-level contractors.

All information on the target and its value was also explained, particularly on the nuclear weapons problem, and all questions were answered on this potentially hazardous situation. Later on, in the spring of 1975, after AZORIAN was blown in the news media but not yet officially canceled, this team spirit philosophy produced its rewards.

At that time contractor personnel were covertly being offered money—as much as $1500—for stories, but none of the ship's crew succumbed. One man who was on the program as an office employee for four months did talk to the press though, apparently on his own volition. The team spirit concept also drew out of everyone involved an effort above and beyond the call of duty. Several hazardous tasks were performed and nothing extra was sought. Future programs of this nature could profit immensely from an application of the team spirit approach to security.

Security personnel handled almost all the briefings of people, both government and industrial, coming onto the project. The briefings weren't just time-consuming; they were the first aspect of AZORIAN that newcomers encountered, and it was important that they be done right.

Likewise, as people left the program, security officers gave them their final briefing. It was the last and, perhaps, most lasting impression people would have of the project. It, too, had to be done just right. Just one disgruntled individual, either as he came onto the program or as he left, could blow AZORIAN out of the water. It was a tribute to the security officers that no such incident occurred.

During the design and development phase a more commercial flavor was coming into the program, and it became necessary to use individuals with industrial security experience. The program office therefore was staffed with a cadre of security officers for this purpose. Others were hired and integrated into Global Marine and Summa (the successor to Hughes Tool.) The senior commercial security officer on the West Coast became the alter ego for the senior Headquarters security officer. Often these security officers were used as generalists and advisors to give commercial guidance on methods that should be used. The U.S. Government footprint was to be avoided while at the same time the government's seal of approval had to be obtained.

The Crucial 4th of August ExCom Meeting:

The following ExCom meeting on the 4th of August, 1971, proved to be crucial to the life of the project. Packard opened by stating he considered it necessary to terminate AZORIAN because of the risks involved, the escalating costs, and the general budget situation. Nevertheless, he asked someone to brief ExCom with a program status.

That was followed by an extended ExCom discussion concerning the cost growth problem, where cost increases included, for example, modifications to the well area for safety reasons; the design and manufacture of a small mining machine for cover purposes; and other contractor cost increases. More details involved the strained budget status, the anticipated very high intelligence value of the target, and the operational risks. Packard then concluded that the project should be continued for a few months, but that they should consider alternatives in case it was subsequently terminated. This guidance was later expanded to direct a thorough cost review while permitting procurement of long-lead items. However, the keel of the surface ship wouldn't be laid until a further approval was granted.

This ExCom meeting was but the first in a number of recurring occasions in which AZORIAN nearly foundered over cost increases and operational risks. Some of the original recovery concepts such as buoyancy lift had been price-tagged low compared to how the chosen concept was first estimated in 1970. However, in less than a year its cost had jumped by more than 50 percent, and another year brought the figure even higher. Each time, however, consideration of the intelligence potential for the project carried the day.

Design and Development of the AZORIAN System:

By the following November of 1971 ExCom meeting, substantial strides had been made in the design and engineering development of the major ship systems, such as the heavy-lift and heave-compensation systems. All the details of the pipe-string design had also been completed, and a pipe-string specimen had been fabricated to develop confidence for pipe section fabrication.

Figure 3. The first stage of construction - laying down the docking well gates.

Designs for the large test fixture which would proof test every 30-foot section of the pipe were now nearly complete. By the fall of 1971 Sun Shipbuilding and Drydock Co., Chester, Pa., which was selected to build the surface ship, had proceeded with the fabrication of the docking well-gate guides and the temporary bottom structure for the docking well, and was preparing to lay the keel. (Figure 3.)

On the 4th of October Packard authorized to proceed with AZORIAN but directed that every effort be made to contain all costs within the then-refined total program cost that was authorized earlier. The work on hardware for all the major elements of the system had started at the same time the engineering specifications were being completed. All data-processing functional requirements were defined and documented during December of 1971, and the configuration of shipboard computers and associated peripheral equipment was put into a final form in January of 1972. The misc. equipment, control center, sensors, and control, power, and data-transmission subsystems had already been completed.

In April of 1972 it was reported to ExCom that the keel for the surface ship had been laid by Sun Shipbuilders on the 16th of November, 1971, and that the schedule now called for a launch by the 5th of October, 1972—with delivery to the program by the 20th of April, 1973. All long-lead equipment was also under procurement and on schedule.

The construction barge was launched in San Diego during January of 1972, and reached Redwood City early in May (This portion is further explained later in this book).

Managerial View of the Program in 1972:

At the ExCom meeting on the 28th of July, 1972, it was pointed out that AZORIAN had been developed as a one-of-a-kind system intended for a specific job, and that because of this uniqueness with the need to accomplish this mission at the earliest possible time, work on the system was proceeding concurrent with both design and production. The consequence had been that amassing this considerable body of knowledge actually enhanced the chances for success, but it also necessitated some costly changes along the way. While they expected delivery of the ship in the spring of 1973 and operational deployment to be in the summer of 1974, it was pointed out that recent major changes had again driven up the total cost for the system. These changes included a ship's hull strengthening, modification to the propulsion shafting, an increased electrical capacity, the incorporation of a sewage system to meet new ecological standards, and an improved pipe-string handling process. In addition, a second and more expensive subcontractor was brought into pipe-string production to meet the tight delivery schedule. However construction of the whole AZORIAN system was still expected to be largely completed by the end of 1973.

Early Political Feasibility Evaluation:

At the 28th of July 1972 ExCom meeting, it was agreed that the 40 Committee should be asked for an early evaluation of the political feasibility of conducting the mission in mid-1974, in light of increased concerns that the developing political climate might prohibit a mission approval by that time (The 40 Committee was responsible for reviewing every covert operation undertaken by the U.S. Government). On the 14th of August, 1972, Kenneth Rush, who had succeeded David Packard as Deputy Secretary of Defense and thereby as chairman of ExCom, forwarded two documents to the 40 Committee, one an intelligence reevaluation of the submarine target object by the ad hoc Committee of USIB, the other a summary of the program's technical, operational, cover, and security factors. He reported to the 40 Committee in his covering memorandum that AZORIAN was still proceeding on schedule. But in light of the developing political climate and uncertain budget problems, he said, ExCom was requesting that this preliminary political assessment be made.

On the 15th of August 1972 Rush forwarded copies of three memoranda relative to the AZORIAN assessment which he'd received from the Chief of Naval Operations, Admiral Elmo R. Zumwalt, Jr.; the Assistant Secretary of Defense (Intelligence), Dr. Hall; and DIA Director Vice Admiral de Poix. All three to varying degrees judged that the value of the anticipated intelligence gain from the mission was less than that estimated by the ad hoc Committee, pointed to the escalating costs and political risks of AZORIAN, and generally felt that the program should be terminated. Zumwalt, while not recommending immediate termination, stated his strong reservations about continuing AZORIAN and recommended that the cost-benefits be studied further with relation to the total DoD intelligence program.

A detailed report was forwarded to Hall which discussed in detail the expected benefits potentially derivable from the recovery of the K-129 target object. It was clear that odds were still favorable as far as the expected mission intelligence value was concerned.

All these papers and the assessment of the ad hoc Committee of USIB reaffirming the expected important intelligence gains—including those in the cryptographic areas—were forwarded to the 40 Committee by Deputy Secretary Rush on the 21st of August 1972 along with CIA comments which took issue with Zumwalt's and Hall's memoranda. At this crucial juncture Admiral Moorer, Chairman of the Joint Chiefs of Staff, sent a memo to the 40 Committee on the 28th of August stating that he couldn't support the proposed AZORIAN mission, primarily because of the decreased intelligence value of the target with the passage of time since K-129 had sunk back in March of 1968, the escalating costs which he believed would continue, and the possibility of a strong reaction from the Soviets if they suspected the nature of this recovery activity.

But Helms countered on the 14th of September with a memo to the Chairman, 40 Committee, which argued for a continuation of AZORIAN. While agreeing that the different judgments around the community concerning the intelligence value of the items and systems believed to be aboard K-129 was understandable in such a difficult program, Helms urged a decision to proceed based on the documentation prepared by the joint program organization and the USIB ad hoc Committee assessment, which he considered an accurate national evaluation on intelligence potential. He further believed that the technical risks were acceptable in view of the expected intelligence value retrieved, and that a political judgment on whether to proceed with the mission could be made satisfactorily only at mission time. He also believed that the risk of a further significant cost increase was low, and that costs recoverable if the program were terminated early would be small.

Then on the 18th of September, 1972, Rush weighed in with his judgment. Because of the current and continuing political relationships and negotiations with the Soviet Union, he believed it was undesirable to execute AZORIAN as was planned. He predicted the Soviets would react strongly with physical force if they learned about the nature of the mission beforehand, and even if they discovered its nature only at a later date, U.S.-Soviet relationships and negotiations would be seriously damaged. He also believed there was a high risk for technical failure, and estimated the chances of technical success at only being 20 to 30 percent based on the existing program schedule and budget. Rush didn't take issue with Helms' evaluation of the intelligence benefits but believed that, overall, the program should be terminated in view of the high political and technical risks. He shared Helms' concern about the effects of a termination on contractor relationships, because the major contractors had publicly committed themselves to a large ocean mining endeavor. Helms felt that a termination now would appear capricious to contractors and jeopardize future cooperative efforts with the intelligence community when contractor support would be needed most.

The AZORIAN Review Panel:

Rush made the next major move by establishing a panel under Hall to review and refine the AZORIAN cost data, to examine the projected savings if the program was cancelled, and, alternatively, to look at any technical risk areas that he believed might lead to greater costs; he also invited Helms to provide a panel member.

The AZORIAN Review Panel consisted of representatives of the DCI, Office of the Science Advisor to the President, a Defense Contract Audit Agency, and the Office of the Assistant Secretary of Defense (Comptroller), and was convened by Helms and Rush.

The panel reported back to Rush on the 11th of December, 1972. By way of background, the report stated that the program had been organized around four major developmental tasks, and that program management had been highly effective with the result that all key phases of the program were on schedule. The key phases included developments that were on the boundary of the state-of-the-art, such as some of the largest forgings ever made, entirely new pipe metallurgy, and a lifting apparatus that couldn't be fully tested prior to the actual mission operation.

These new and dramatic developments led to some legitimate concerns about the future technological risks they faced. In the time available the panel couldn't examine the program's technical uncertainties, but stated that such a bold engineering undertaking must be considered a high-risk venture.

The panel also concluded:

1. The possible savings to the government if AZORIAN was terminated early.
2. Should the program be continued, the estimated cost growth going forward.
3. The current schedule allows for the mission to be executed on the target date.
4. They can't test the full system in advance of the actual lift operation.
5. Engineering unknowns were proving to be the greatest uncertainty to the program.

In a separate report on the 21st of November, 1972, a member of the AZORIAN Review Panel concluded that as a result of this overview of the project, the technical prognosis was good, project management remained excellent, with schedule and cost aspects tracking reasonably well. He noted that the project was then entering a critical testing phase wherein difficulties had to be expected despite anticipatory efforts having been exerted to date. He believed that further cost growth would probably develop during the testing phase, but some substantial offsets could be generated as well.

Regarding costs—it was noted that the total project cost had grown by 66 percent to what was estimated in October of 1970 based on contractor proposals, and by another six percent from what the contracts were calculating in December of 1971. Considering the highly developmental nature of the undertaking, he regarded this as a creditable performance. AZORIAN, he said, was clearly a bold engineering undertaking which staggered the imagination. It reflected a massive degree of concurrency in design, development, and production, and—being without precedent in its totality—must be considered a high-risk venture. Each element of the total system, however, was given highly professional scientific and engineering attention, and thorough testing routines were planned short of the final operation.

The 40 Committee Decision to Proceed:

The ExCom decision to seek a 40 Committee review culminated on the 11th of December, 1972. After the most intensive, detailed, and broad-based examination to date of all the facets with the program, the final decision, made by the President, was to continue the AZORIAN project, with 40 Committee exercising the appropriate policy supervision.

In his memo on that date to 40 Committee principals, Dr. Kissinger said the President was impressed by the project's creative and innovative approach to a complicated task and that he praised the cooperation among elements of the intelligence community to serve this national objective.

Almost four years after the initial discussions between Agency and DoD representatives about the feasibility of recovering the K-129 submarine, a very crucial milestone had been passed, the most important in a long series of high-level program reviews which, at times, had threatened the continued existence of the AZORIAN program. Now, with the Presidential green light, the program office redoubled its efforts to keep all work and planning on schedule to maximize the chances for program success.

1972 Work Continues:

The builders of the heavy lift system were well into testing components and systems during the spring and summer of 1972. When one of the lifting yokes failed under a proof load, metallurgical and structural investigation of the failure dictated a change from the T-1 steel specified by the designers to the more forgiving HY-100 steel. The tests surfaced this problem in time for two new HY-100 yokes to be built and delivered to the ship for installation without seriously disrupting the schedule.

Other major equipment was arriving at the Sun Shipyard by the fall of 1972 for installation as the hull neared completion. On the 4th of November, 1972, the ship was launched, installed briefly in drydock to have her false bottom removed and the well-gates installed, then tied dockside for resumption of equipment installation. (Figures 4 through 10 depict construction activities during this period.)

Figure 4. Wing walls going up from the gates and forming the sides of the docking well.

The intense activity at the Chester, Pa. shipyard and the pace of related construction programs were reviewed weekly by the managers meeting in nearby Philadelphia, where they charted current progress, determined what corrections were necessary, and passed these on to all the program managers.

Figure 5. Interior construction looking forward from the stern.

After each session, more detailed scheduling meetings were held the next day at the shipyard to focus on the progress and problems with the HGE's construction.

Figure 6. The bow in final stages of construction.

Hardware Acquisition:

While management was preparing material for the never-ending reviews of the program, security was being burdened by a never-ending demand for security access approvals from contractors. Hardware acquisition was beginning, and that meant even more personnel involvement; operating crews for the Glomar Explorer were being recruited, and still more background investigations were required.

Figure 7. A view of the stern showing the twin propellers.

All this was being done by the Office of Security without exposing government interest. To add to the load, the Agency's technical, planning, and contracting officers were traveling more frequently to visit contractors. The work schedules had to be met; yet face-to-face meetings were required.

It also wouldn't do for the contractors to continually troop into Washington, D.C. The Agency people had to visit the contractors at their home plants or at neutral meeting places. Stringent security measures were required to permit these activities to occur without damaging cover. Every detail had to be examined in order to mask the government's presence.

Figure 8. Final hull work including the painting.

Security also provided support of all types at the meetings that took place in cities all over the country. No tasks were too small or ignorable if it meant protection for AZORIAN. Many of these meetings were attended by very senior government officials as well as by senior corporate officials, some of whom were closely allied with Howard Hughes. The cover would never have held if meetings between officials at this level had become public knowledge. Rooms, apartments, and meeting places were obtained. Security officers acted as the chauffeurs while getting the high and mighty, as well as the not-so-high and mighty, to meetings.

Figure 9. Almost ready for the launching ceremony.

They served as caterers too, providing a food service so that meetings could continue through all the lunch and dinner hours when necessary. Security handled the glamorous with aplomb, the mundane with professionalism, and the trivial with a smile.

Besides the steady flow of people around the country, there was also a cascade of documents that required movement. In the government world, there were the usual security classification stamps. To move all these documents securely among the many contractor and government offices was an onerous task. This was made worse by the spate of aircraft hijackings that took place in the early 1970's. Security officers spent many hours in order to keep the information moving. The ability to move documents almost immediately was one more factor which helped to keep the program on schedule.

Hardware Testing:

As the hardware took shape and became pieces of operating equipment, this equipment had to be tested, and government employees would be heavily involved in all aspects of the testing phase. They'd be in charge of the at-sea operations and also become members of the various working crews. Then there was the essential equipment to be loaded aboard which couldn't stand public scrutiny. For each problem encountered, the security officers devised a successful solution. For those going aboard the Glomar Explorer, it was the sea itself that also offered protection. Equipment that needed protection from disclosure was always put on the ship in a secure way.

Government visitors to the ship during the at-sea testing phase moved under the constant and watchful eye of security officers. And an extra hazard during the testing phase eventually tried security's mettle. This was the labor strife at the pier stemming from the Marine Engineers Beneficial Association's attempt to unionize the crews working for Global Marine. The Global Marine management people were adamantly opposed to unionization, and the case went to the

National Labor Relations Board (NLRB), which scheduled hearings and pondered whether to conduct a union shop election among Global Marine's employees.

Figure 10. Sliding down the ways.

The hearing process was long, tedious, and full of delays, and all the while CIA had to walk a tightrope and maintain a neutral posture. Global Marine was notorious for its swift firing of employees who didn't meet management's strict standards, and some of the Glomar Explorer's crew were union sympathizers; on the other hand, unionization of GMI at this stage, and the imposition of hiring hall procedures, would complicate the background investigation process and crew selection. For a while the government considered taking the union leaders into its confidence and asking for their help in preserving AZORIAN's security.

Two incidents particularly stretched the security officers' nerves during the proceedings. Early on, the union forces, including some strong-arm types, appeared at the gate to the pier and things got quite tense; the non-union crew members weren't shrinking violets either. The union gang slashed a few tires and threw nails on the roadway, but the security people kept their cool and no fights erupted. Meanwhile, during a recess in the NLRB hearings, some union lawyers were heard to mutter that the deep ocean mining project wasn't what it's purported to be. A union member was able to reassure the alarmed security officers that the comments were just a lot of hot air; there was no problem with the mining project cover.

Finally, as the AZORIAN project neared its completion, the NLRB hearings worked their own way to a conclusion, and Global Marine remained non-unionized. More important to the government, CIA had been able to preserve its involvement from public exposure without affecting the course of the labor negotiations.

By January of 1973 the HGE's engines were running and shore power was disconnected. The 800 tons of gimbal platforms and bearings, which had been concurrently pre-assembled pier-side, were installed on top of the shipboard heave compensation cylinders by using the Sun 800 barge crane (Figures 11 thru 15).

The Sun 800 was specially constructed by Sun just for this lift, and was the largest capacity (800 tons) barge crane on the East Coast. Later, because the ship's derrick was too tall to pass under the Delaware Memorial Bridge, this crane followed the HGE downriver to set the derrick aboard after the ship had cleared the bridge.

Figure 11. A-frame structure which provided the load path from the lift system to the ship.

This was a busy time and the HQ engineering representatives found themselves more often at the shipyard than anywhere else. The magnitude and complexity of the installations were greater than the initial shipyard estimates —more manpower with more time was being consumed.

Continued meetings were held with shipyard management in an effort to keep the electricians, pipe fitters, mechanics, welders, and their foremen working aboard the HGE in the face of stiff competition from other ships also under construction. It required the clearance and briefing of a Sun Shipyard vice president (he was also the production manager) to improve the situation.

Figure 12. Aft heave compensator cylinder. This is one of the shock absorbers which removed the up-and-down motion of the ship from the recovery mechanism.

During February and March of 1973, the installation of the major recovery system component plumbing, wiring, and lift system control equipment continued. The docking legs were installed and welded. The rig floor had been installed and was receiving equipment for the draw works. Coast Guard representatives were following all these activities. Tie-down castings were installed in the well floor. These would later be changed to weldments because the porous castings absorbed leakage from well-gate ballast. The balance of effort in the shipyard was devoted to the dock trials of the basic ship's systems in preparation for the builder's sea trials to happen on the 12th of April.

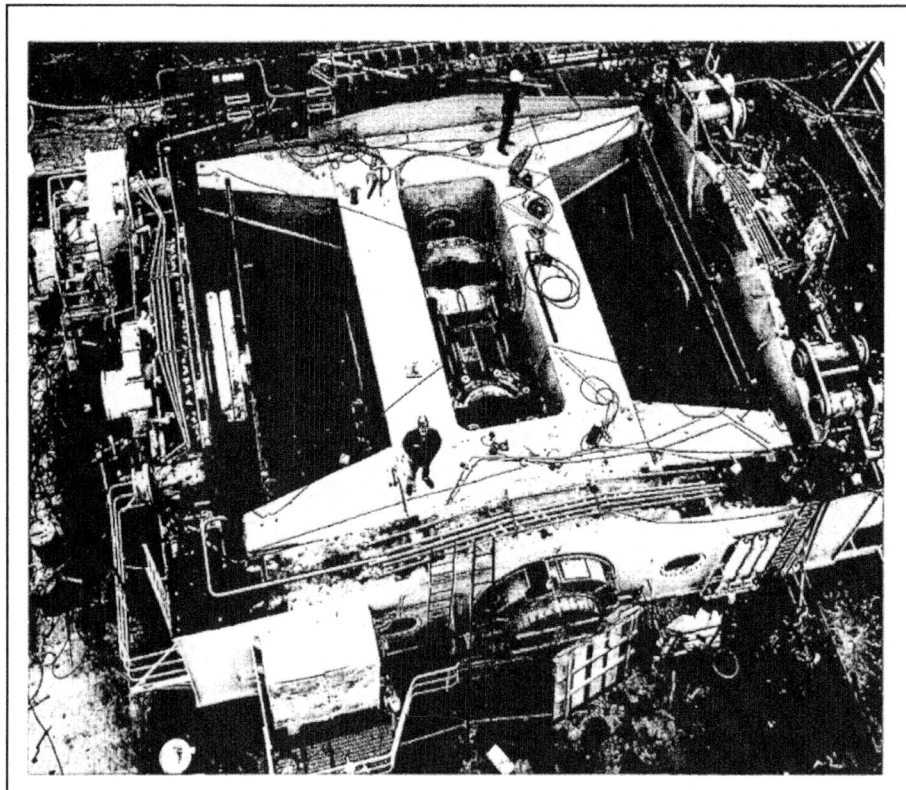

Figure 13. Inner and outer gimbals which removed the roll and pitch motion.

The period after the builder's trials (which were successful in demonstrating the intended basic ship's systems) from mid-April to the 24th of July 1973 marked the completion of the recovery system installation and the initiation of the dock trials. (Figure 16.)

After extensive hydro-testing to 4500 pounds per square inch and rework, the heave compensation system held pressure. The piston rods with their yokes supporting the 800 tons of gimbal platforms and lift system finally made the

15-foot trip up the guides from full low to a full high position and back down again. The heave compensation system had also completed dockside checkout.

Figure 14. Gimbals being set on the A-frame.

Like the heave compensation system, the heavy lift system required several cycles of hydro-testing, repair, and retest before the system held pressure. The flanged joints turned into a particular concern. Their surfaces had to be perfectly machined and aligned in order to hold the proof test pressure of 4500 psi.

Figure 15. The barge crane, Sun 800, lifting on the prefabricated aft deck house.

After considerable rework, this system held pressure and was ready for a final dockside test. Finally both sets of the lift cylinders with their rods and yokes were stroked for 15 feet, but not without damage to the upper yoke. An out-of-sync condition between the two piston rods caused the yoke to tilt and bear against one of the rods. Metallurgical and structural assessment showed the damage was repairable and the yoke stiffener plate was repaired in place.

With completion of the stroking, the lift system testing had progressed as far as was feasible while the HGE was still dockside. Also not much shipyard testing was done on the pipe handling system because of the intensive shipyard activity on the other systems. In fact, there was nothing more at all that could be done in the yard, and the HGE departed the Sun Shipyard on the 24th of July, 1973, for further sea trials. Construction of this remarkable ship had been completed in the equally remarkable time of 20 months since first laying the keel.

Figure 16. The final product.

The story of the construction of the HGE wouldn't be complete without skipping ahead 15 months to October of 1974 and the preparations for the follow-on mission code-named MATADOR. AZORIAN had fully tested the basic design of the surface ship's system. Although the equipment would incur many problems during the recovery mission, nothing had faulted the soundness of the basic design. What was further needed was the repair of damaged hardware and engineering improvements—fine tuning of the major sub-systems, if you will—in order to make the over-all operation run more smoothly and trouble-free. This was especially true in the heavy lift system, and to a much lesser degree in the pipe handling system.

Meanwhile the HGE herself had come through with flying colors. All that she required was a facelift—a cleaning and painting of the hull—after a thorough non-destructive inspection with some minor repairs. The MATADOR test operations were very successful and proved the value of these modifications.

HGE Technology and Cost:

The HGE and her associated sub-systems created a number of significant technical achievements and breakthroughs. The ship was the first one to be designed and analyzed using finite element analysis (approved by the American Bureau of Shipping). She had the largest (199 feet by 74 feet) center well with movable gates. The 24,500 horsepower diesel electric marine power system was the largest built that used 4100-volt alternating current coupled to silicone-controlled rectifiers. The use of jack-up type legs, derived from the offshore oil industry, as the docking mechanism solved the problem of mating two massive bodies in a seaway and was an important breakthrough.

The heavy lift system was the largest and most powerful (8000 tons) lift system ever built. The pipe handling system was the largest automatic one in use and could store and assemble 60-foot pipe sections averaging about 15 tons each. The heave compensator and gimbal platforms were the largest in the offshore industry. They supported 10,000 tons which isolated them hydraulically and pneumatically from the ship's motion. This in turn permitted precise bottom operations to be carried out with highly accurate positioning while the surface ship was responding to wave and wind forces.

The World's Largest Submersible:

The Hughes Mining Barge-1, known as the HMB-1, was to become the world's largest submersible. During its construction in San Diego, President Nixon was photographed in front of it giving a speech about our U.S. Government support to the American shipbuilding industry. This presidential publicity for the HMB-1 wasn't planned as a part of the cover program, and the Agency received only 24 hours advance notice for the visit. Fortunately, no undue attention to AZORIAN resulted from the photograph and speech, which became featured in many newspapers at that time.

HMB-1 Requirements:

The HMB-1 had to meet three main requirements. First, it was to serve as the facility for the covert construction of the capture vehicle (CV). The CV was so large it couldn't be built within the well of the HGE. Even if that was possible, management couldn't wait until the HGE was completed to begin construction of the CV because the required schedules were so tight. And since any public exposure of the CV would blow the mining cover, it had to be built beyond the reaches of the prying eyes of news reporters; therefore the construction facility had to be fully enclosed and protected. Second, because the CV and the HGE were built at separate facilities, the CV would need to be transported to a mating site; so the enclosed construction site had to be movable. Third, a covert method of transferring the CV into the HGE was needed; the construction facility, therefore, had to be submersible to a depth at which the HGE could moor over it and extract the CV, concealed by the intervening water. In any case, the HGE itself was the only device powerful enough to lift the CV's weight of 1600 tons (wet).

HMB-1 Construction:

Building a barge is normally a straightforward process involving uncomplicated structures. A barge is a floating box, and the HMB-1, when surfaced, wasn't overly complex (Figure 17). But it had to be submersible, with hard and soft tanks being needed for flooding in order to change the buoyancy of the submersible barge. (Hard tanks are built to withstand external pressure; soft tanks are pressure-equalized.) Floodable stabilizing cylinders were also added to control diving and surfacing operations.

Figure 17. HMB-1 on the ways.

Fabrication began on the 11th of May, 1971, with the laying down of the stern soft tanks. Construction progressed from stern to bow and keel to roof in several planned stages.

The necessary submersible complexities didn't hinder the construction process, and it progressed ahead rapidly. Lockheed completed the movable roof design and removed their engineers to prepare for test procedures with dock and sea trials. The last structural items, the bow, roof sections, and stabilizing tanks, were completed by early April of 1972. Then on the 14th of April the hull was launched and placed at the outfitting dock (Figures 18 and 19). Here the roof sections and stabilizing cylinders were added. Onboard outfitting of the control rooms, roof drives, anchor windlasses, instrumentation and aft bulkhead were completed within a week. The HMB-1 was now ready to prove itself as the world's largest submersible.

Figure 18. She floats!

Various sites had previously been surveyed for the necessary sea trials. Requirements were a smooth and sandy bottom, a gradual slope (at less than three degrees), and sufficient water depth for progressive testing to about 185 feet. Two sites were eventually chosen to be used.

Figure 19. The HMB-1 being outfitted at the dock.

The first was off Coronado Island in San Diego. The water depth was 55 feet, which meant that the crew, procedures, and barge could be tested without a full submergence, and it was close enough in case problems were uncovered. The second site was Isthmus Cove at Catalina Island. Here there was sufficient water depth to check the barge at 125 feet, 165 feet and 182 feet.

On the 20th of April, 1972, which was 11 months after construction began, the HMB-1 headed for its first dive off Coronado Island. After the anchors and buoys were set and all pre-dive checkouts were made, HMB-1 started down (Figure 20). By late evening it was nestled on the bottom. No major problems were found, and the next morning it resurfaced. The following day, on the 22nd of April, the tow to Catalina Island began. By the 24th of April the small test flotilla was anchored in place and ready to begin a series of four dives—twice to 125 feet, once to 165 feet, and a final dive to 182 feet.

Figure 20. Getting ready for a dive at Catalina. The support barge is at the right, the tow boat is on the left.

The dives were conducted between the 24th of April and the 10th of May. On the first dive, air remaining in the barge collected under the roof as it descended; and almost as quickly as it had gone down, the top of HMB-1 appeared back at the surface. Then as the remaining trapped air vented out through holes in the roof, negative buoyancy returned and it dropped to the bottom again. This yo-yo effect was overcome in subsequent dives by blowing the ballast tanks to insure that the HMB-1 remained negatively buoyant throughout the dive sequence.

There were minor, correctable problems with the next two dives, but on the fourth dive a really tough issue appeared when a float valve in the starboard control room closed, shutting down the constant air supply essential to the operation of the barge's instruments, including the valve controls by which buoyancy was regulated. The HMB-1 lay dead at the bottom, unable to respond, until divers were sent down into the control room to operate the valves by hand. The diving sequence proceeded to a successful completion without incident or damage to the barge. The problem was quickly identified: the float valve had reacted to excessive moisture in the compressed air, "identifying" it as water and dutifully closing itself. A design correction erased this problem and on the 10th of May the HMB-1 cleared the test site headed for Redwood City by San Francisco Bay, where it was to become the construction hanger for the capture vehicle.

HMB-1 Technology:

The HMB-1 contributed its own technical achievements to the AZORIAN program. It was the world's largest submersible in addition to being the construction facility, transport vehicle and covert transfer mechanism for the 2400-ton (dry) capture vehicle.

Another technical accomplishment was the unmanned submergence of this huge barge. A floating vessel goes from positive buoyancy through zero buoyancy to negative buoyancy during the submerging process. At zero buoyancy the vessel is unstable and theoretically could go belly-up at this exact moment. Therefore, it became no small achievement for the HMB-1 to go through this critically unstable point while being unmanned.

The barge construction was finished in 11 months, and after completion of the test dives, it was towed to the Redwood City facility which was to become its home base. It was there, on the 30th of May, 1972, that assembly of the capture vehicle began to happen in total secrecy.

My Darling Clementine:

The one piece of equipment that couldn't bear public scrutiny was the capture vehicle. Its giant arms with davits (forearms) and beams (upper arms) could serve only one purpose—encircling something huge. They deserved their given name, the Grabber System. Although the CV was christened Clementine, no one would ever believe that she was even remotely related to the Miner and Forty-Niner immortalized in a song. The design, therefore, had to be done in secret, as did the assembly. Any failure here would end the cover and end the mission.

To give credence to all the security precautions being taken, Clementine was billed as Howard Hughes' latest engineering marvel. She was the key to making him even richer by efficiently harvesting the manganese nodules lying on the ocean floor. No one was to see Mr. Hughes' new device. The story was floated, believed, and served as the perfect cover. No unauthorized individuals ever saw Clementine.

"The Claw is in the Bay" was the headline splashed across the front page of a local newspaper when the HMB-1 first appeared in the San Francisco Bay area. What a surprise it must've been to the writers when they found out later how close their headline actually was; not to the Claw, the local nickname for Howard Hughes, but to a not so dainty lady named Clementine.

CV Requirements:

The CV, like the HGE, had detailed lists of design requirements for each of its major elements, as well as all of its many subsystems. Strength requirements for the various load-carrying structures were defined, total system weights were carefully estimated since the lift-off weight was a critical factor in mission success, and controls for setting the massive CV down on the target were exactingly specified to achieve an accuracy of placement within one foot. The alignment would involve two massive objects (each the weight of a light destroyer), one of which would be remotely controlled at the end of a flexible pipe string. Using analogies to help grasp the complexity of the task aren't completely satisfactory. However, imagine standing on the top of the Empire State Building with a four by eight-foot grappling device attached to one end of a one-inch diameter steel rope. The task is to lower the rope and grapple to the street below, snag a compact-sized car full of gold (for weight simulation, not necessarily value) and pull the car back up to the top of the building, with the job being done without anyone taking notice of it. Mission Impossible?—one might think so.

    The structures and mechanisms of the CV had to provide the mechanical features necessary to seize the target on the bottom, free it from the surrounding muck, and hold on to it and lift it to the surface, and place it within the HGE. The same mechanical features also had to have the capability of disposing of the submarine at sea after it had been gutted, analyzed and stripped of the secrets. Other design requirements of the CV system involved sensors and controls which provided the necessary navigation and status information for operational decision-making. Two complex electromechanical cables tied the CV with the control center and were part of the CV's system requirement package, as was the control center itself.

The CV arrangements were designed with personnel safety as the prime requirement. Concerns for personal safety were high in the designers' minds because of the massive size of the equipment that was to be handled at sea on a rolling and pitching ship. Plus divers would have to work around the CV during the deployment operation. Next in the designers' priority list came satisfaction of the functional requirements, followed by protection from damage, accessibility, with minimum complexity and minimum structural foundations. A useful life of three years was the design goal for all of the components and subsystems. The CV wasn't to exceed 4,929,000 pounds dry weight or 3,300,000 pounds weight in water and was required to withstand 10 exposures to 16,700 feet and survive for 500 hours of continuous operation at this depth.

CV Construction:

The prime contractor selected to build the CV system was the Lockheed Missile and Space Company (LMSC). They were selected for three main reasons: their Ocean Systems Division had considerable experience in building submersibles, LMSC had shown good system engineering methodology in their aerospace efforts, and they were long and successfully experienced in running "black" programs. The latter was particularly important because the success of the cover story hinged on keeping the CV in the "black." LMSC had the ability to go to a wide range of subcontractors without letting them in on the true story. For example, the backbone of the CV was constructed by the U.S. Steel's American Bridge Division in South San Francisco. The steel for the beams and davits was supplied by Allegheny Ludlum in the East; they were fabricated at the Kaiser-Fontana steel works in Southern California. One major subcontractor to LMSC was brought into the black side of the program. Honeywell's Marine System Division in Seattle was given the contract for the electromechanical cable and all the sonars and controls for the CV.

The CV system was broken down into three elements; the CV element, the electronics element, and the construction barge element, the last being the HMB-1 already described earlier. The CV element was the principal structural and mechanical assembly of the CV system. The electronics element provided the CV element with electrical power, sensors, and controls.

Within the CV element, the hull structure served as the primary load-carrying member. Originally it was designed as a truss and girder structure. When this design ran into a problem, a "tiger team" from Kelly Johnson's U-2 skunk works was put together to come up with an alternative plan. As a result of this effort, a much lighter box beam design was put forward and approved. It used a relatively new bridge steel, T-1, with a yield strength of 100,000 pounds per square inch (Figures 21 and 22).

This box beam design, called the strongback, turned into the world's largest single weldment structure. Some of the welds required as many as 250 passes to complete. The hull structure contained a 15 by 17-foot opening to allow pipe to be deployed while the CV was carried in the HGE's well. It also was compartmented for ballasting. This meant that the CV could be adjusted 0.6 degree and 2.5 degrees in list and trim, respectively, for docking operations. The hull structure also carried all the sensors, propulsion units, and the electronics spheres and cabling.

Attached to the hull were the four massive bottom setting legs, 12 feet in diameter with 15 by 16-foot rectangular foot pads (Figure 23). Each leg had an inner cylinder which could be extended 35 feet at a rate of 1.5 feet per minute using hydraulic pressure from sea water pumped down the pipe string. These legs could develop a total lift of 5,740,000 pounds which was to be used to extract the target out of the sticky bottom soil. Once the target was broken off of the bottom, all four legs would be dropped off—their connector pins pulled hydraulically—to reduce the critical lift-off weight.

Figure 21. Strongback being loaded on the HMB-1 at the Ambridge plant in South San Francisco.

Also attached to the barge's hull structure were the eight beams and davits (called grabbers) for encircling and holding the submarine hull just like a set of gigantic tongs. There were five on the port side and three on the starboard side of the CV. The beams and davits were fabricated from maraging 200, a high nickel steel. This steel had the property of high strength per unit weight of material, which was necessary to keep the over-all weight of the CV within the design goal. (Unfortunately, the nickel gave the maraging 200 steel ductility characteristics which proved to be insufficient during the recovery operation.) Each grabber had a design load limit of 1,340,000 pounds or about 600 long tons. The safety factor was 1.5—the grabber could take 1.5 times its design load before failing, for a total load capacity of 900 long tons per grabber. In the event that the target object strength or geometry precluded any single grabber from carrying its share of the load, the spacing was designed so that the added load on the adjacent grabber wouldn't reduce the safety factor below 1.15.

Figure 22. Strongback shored up in the HMB-1 and ready for outfitting.

Seawater pumped down the center of the lift pipe (maximum rate 1,240 gallons per minute at 3,000 psi above ambient) provided power for the eight large thrusters mounted on the hull of the CV. These thrusters plus two small electrically driven units provided the forces necessary to maneuver the CV and accurately position it over the target for the delicate set-down operation. The pumped seawater was also used to drape a chain net under and around the No.

1 missile tube on the submarine target. Its purpose was to contain, support and prevent the loss of the almost severed tube and its missile contents during breakout and lift.

The CV was attached to the heavy lift pipe by the bridle assembly. This was made from pieces of the small-diameter heavy lift pipe. The apex assembly (the flexible joint between the bridle and the pipe) was made from maraging 200 steel forgings. These were the largest components ever made from this type of steel. The design load for the bridle itself was 9,460,000 pounds. It was stowed in a collapsed position on the CV hull and erected as the CV was lowered on the docking legs.

Figure 23. One of Clementine's feet.

The electronics element was the third major portion of the CV system. This element, including its array of sensors, provided control of all the electromechanical and hydraulic CV equipment, navigation data for determining position and attitude of the CV, imaging of the target object and the surrounding bottom terrain, and status monitoring of the hydraulic and mechanical equipment. There were long-range sonars, high-resolution sonars, altitude/attitude sonars and 11 TV cameras with 22 lights providing the "eyes" for the CV. Target capture could be achieved with either the acoustic or the optic system independently. A beacon transponder array carried on the CV was also deployed around the target. Interrogation of this array by hydrophones on the CV allowed the CV to be positioned with an accuracy of one foot at a range up to 500 feet from the transponders. Maneuvering controls took data from all the sonars and automatically executed commands to the thrusters, thereby controlling the CV's heading to within ± five feet in surge and ± two and one-half feet in sway.

Two fully redundant electromechanical cables comprised the transmission portion of the electronics element. These cables were 18,500 feet in length and were the first things to be manufactured. The cables handled the ship's power provided at 2000 volts, three phase, and 60 cycles. They also provided up and down-link telemetry channels, a video data channel and an acoustic sensor data channel. A minimum of 9,600 bits of information per second could be handled. The electrical network was designed in such a way that no single equipment or circuit failure could cause mission abort or failure.

The final portion of the electronics element was the control center aboard the ship. It provided the working space for the Mission Director, the Deputy for Handling, the Deputy for Recovery and one assistant, the CV operator, CV work systems operator, optics equipment operator and two acoustic equipment operators. Each station contained the necessary displays and controls to operate all of the CV equipment. Three vans made up this complex, which also served as the focal point for secure communications to the forward pilot house, aft pilot house, heavy lift control center, the divers and the ship's center well.

After the major assembly of the CV was completed, it was given a final dry test at Redwood City. This test was completed on the 30th of June, 1973. Prior to this test exhaustive engineering, evaluation and factory acceptance tests were run on components and subassemblies. The engineering team that built the CV and would eventually operate it was, for all intents and purposes, in permanent residence at the Redwood City facility. By the time the CV left the San Francisco Bay area for mating with the HGE, all construction had been completed except for a final rigging of the beams and davits. The full area of the HGE's well was needed for this final readiness activity to prepare Clementine for testing and recovery operations (Figures 24 and 25).

Figure 24. Clementine inside the HGE. Outfitting is almost completed. On the left note the chain net used to contain the missile tube on the Soviet submarine.

CV Technology:

The CV system contributed a number of technical achievements in its evolution from design to reality. The electromechanical cable pushed hard against the state-of-the-art in high-strength, long-length, low-diameter, and low-attenuation undersea cables. This cable carried a digital data link used for the first time to control and precisely maneuver a very large machine suspended at the end of a flexible drill pipe.

Figure 25. Clementine with her bridle readied for use.

The bottom reference system allowed deep operating equipment to be positioned with an unheard-of accuracy of one foot. At the same time, the automatic station-keeping system provided positioning of the large HGE to within only

± 15 feet. The CV itself had a hull which wasn't only the largest structure made from T-1 steel, but was also the world's largest single weldment.

The deep sea hydraulic legs of about 1000-ton capacity were unique, as was the pressure-compensated electrical system. Finally, the spider and apex block (the flexible top portion of the bridle) were the largest components ever machined from maraging steel forgings.

Hanging By A Thread:

There was clearly a single-point failure mechanism built into the approved recovery scheme—it was the heavy lift pipe. Because if it failed, not only would the mission end abruptly, but major damage would also be done to the HGE. The sudden release of energy to the upper portion of the pipe string would create havoc on the drill floor and cause severe injury to the men operating it from above. The pipe had to be designed with a good safety margin, and it had to be built perfectly. Tight quality control and proof testing would be mandatory. The Hughes Tool Company was selected as the primary contractor for this critical portion of the hardware. It would be almost inconceivable that a Hughes-sponsored mining adventure wouldn't use its own company, the Hughes Tool Company, to provide the drill pipe.

These pioneers in the oil field and mining supply business had extensive experience at manufacturing drill bits and had a thorough knowledge of pipe machining and metallurgy. Hughes Tool Company brought the right combination of technical expertise and cover logic.

Pipe String Requirements:

The principal requirement on the heavy lift pipe was to provide enough strength to lift the target object and the CV while sustaining its own weight and any dynamic forces added from sea motion. Early CIA studies had concluded that it wouldn't be possible to manufacture a pipe that could meet these strength requirements. Global Marine and Lockheed, after studying the problem, convinced the Agency engineers that the required strength could be achieved, but the proof was still in the making. The maximum estimated load on the pipe was 17,126,00 pounds during fail-safe hold conditions.

Another design requirement of the pipe was specially designed screw threads to hold the pieces of pipe together. The roots of these threads were highly stressed. The design allowed the joint to be made up to a final torque of 300,000 foot-pounds in about one and a half rotations of the pipe. To keep the weight of the pipe string down, it was designed in six diameters varying from 15.5 inches to 12.75 inches. The design also spelled out a protective outer coating—to prevent corrosion from degrading the pipe's strength—and a zinc coating on the threads to lessen the chances of them sticking and galling.

Pipe String Construction:

The closest technology for the pipe string was that used in making 16-inch gun barrels for battleships. Since battleships were all resting in their Valhalla, there was no current 16-inch gun barrel activity to draw upon. But the Army did provide from their Watervliet Arsenal in New York a metallurgist who knew gun barrel technology. The Army brought him to Washington on very short notice and had kept him in the dark about the purpose of the visit. Naturally the specialist became very surprised when two CIA officers picked him up at the Pentagon and took him off for some briefings on the subject. Nobody knew what he was thinking but after hearing a description of the AZORIAN program and the metallurgical problems, the Army metallurgist became very helpful, especially in the evaluation of the manufacturing process and concerning what manufacturers were needed for the pipe.

The Hughes Tool Company next sought out potential contractors to pour, forge, and trepan (cut the center hole in) the rough pieces, with Hughes itself doing the final machining, coating, and proof testing. From the candidate steel companies, they chose (with Agency approval) a company that wasn't currently producing pieces of the required size, but were making smaller gun barrels with the capability for making higher quality steel. When it became clear early on that they couldn't handle the entire load, Jorgensen Steel, with its forging plant in Seattle, was brought in. Later on, as the pressures on the production schedule increased, a third company, National Forge in Erie, Pennsylvania, was hired to complete the production run. These three companies combined delivered a total of 584 rough-machined forgings in 30-foot lengths.

The steel selected to furnish the high strength was formally called AISI 4330V (mod.). This meant that it was a standard, well-known alloy steel that was modified with the addition of vanadium. Vanadium was added to give the proper strength, ductility, and toughness properties to the steel. Its minimum yield strength was 125,000 pounds per square inch. There was much concern over the ability to make forgings of the required size, and at the same time maintain uniformity of material properties throughout the forging, so this process was followed closely by Hughes, Agency engineers, and metallurgical consultants who were hired for their expertise.

Nothing about this single-thread failure mechanism was taken for granted. Several one-eighth scale pieces of pipe were made and subjected to scale model tests. The testing machine was computer-controlled with a program that mimicked the load conditions imposed on the pipe by ocean forces. The goal of the test program was the completion of four life-cycles of testing without indications of fatigue cracking in the specimen (Figures 26 and 27).

Figure 26. A piece of pipe being lowered into the proof test machine.

Figure 27. The Dutchman, the first piece of pipe in the string, under load in the proof test machine.

Each life-cycle was defined as 340,000 individual load cycles, which was equivalent to 940 hours of operation. During testing it was found six life-cycles were successfully completed before fatigue cracking began. These results indicated a high probability that the pipe would successfully survive the estimated operational time (testing plus mission), which was 250,000 cycles or 690 hours.

Figure 28. Pipe at Pier E showing pipe assembled into doubles 60 feet long. Threads are coated with a titanium dioxide/silicon oil coating to prevent seizure.

The final, full-scale proof test of the heavy lift pipe further demonstrated the "take nothing for granted attitude." After Hughes had finished the final machining, coating, and color coding for size, they also subjected each piece to a proof test of 125% of its maximum expected load. This meant that the largest pieces would be loaded to 21,460,000 pounds. To do this required the design and construction of a special proof test machine for the Hughes facility in Houston. Battelle

Memorial Institute in Columbus, Ohio, designed and supervised the construction of the machine.

It became the largest tensile test machine ever built. On the 30th of January, 1972, the design engineer—with much trepidation—initiated the first full-load test of the pipe with the machine. Neither failed. Nor did they ever fail, even once, during the tensile testing of the 584 finished and delivered pieces. This was a fine tribute to the design effort and the quality control that went into the production of the pipe string.

As the pieces were completed in Houston, they were assembled into 60-foot doubles and loaded onto rail cars for shipment to the HGE (Figure 28).

The only refurbishment the heavy lift pipe required for MATADOR—the second mission—was the inspection and retorquing of the joints made up at the factory, and the repair of some minor corrosion pits on the threads.

Pipe String Technology:

The forgings from which the basic pieces were cut were the largest members ever produced to such high strength, ductility, and fracture toughness requirements. Stringent metallurgical controls and inspections were required throughout the manufacturing process.

The large pipe threads had a unique design which accommodated a high-load capacity simultaneously with a quick make/break connection. The proof test machine was the largest in the world. It had a maximum load capacity of 24,000,000 pounds.

The pipe string was designed, built, tested, and delivered in a 29 1/2 month period from the 29th of May, 1971, to the 15th of October, 1973. Forging and machining required 21 1/2 months, testing 8 months, and deliveries took place over the last 7 months. All pieces were at the pier well before the first sea trials took place in January of 1974.

Data Handling:

A relatively small but important item was the data processing system. It was developed by the Marine System Division of Honeywell, Inc. under a covert contract from the U.S. Government. Honeywell had other key parts of the AZORIAN hardware, including the station keeping and the sonar systems, but they were done as subcontracts to Global Marine and Lockheed. The main requirement on the data processing system was to have all the data logging and retrieval, plus the control of the HGE and the CV, operated from a single, centrally located computer facility. The system that was developed was a complex multi-computer system used for both the on-line control of shipboard machinery and off-line data processing functions. The system consisted of six ruggedized computers each with 32K of core memory, along with related peripherals such as magnetic tapes, disk packs, alphanumeric CRT displays, card readers and punch, line printers, and plotters.

Primary functions of the system were the control of the vessel's position (automatic station keeping), the coordinated control of underwater machinery, and data logging and retrieval. For example, the automatic station keeping routine used data from the heavy lift system and the ship's basic instrumentation to calculate the movements required to position the ship correctly in relation to the target. The results of these calculations could be fed directly into the ship's controls, causing the ship to maneuver without the need for human hands.

Of special interest were the operational support programs. One was used to help track the intelligence material retrieved from the target. Another was a weather applications program which predicted the response of the HGE and the CV, as well as the stresses in the heavy lift pipe resulting from weather induced sea conditions. Still another program calculated the adjustments needed in the anchor chains of the HGE to align her over the HMB-1 for mate/demating operations. This was undoubtedly the most precise four-point moor of any major ship at the time.

A training simulator was also built as a part of the data processing system. It consisted of a movable array of lights and miniature TV cameras to represent those on the CV. A software program was developed to simulate motion, forces, movement, and other information that would be coming to the control center operators during the actual recovery operation. Using a model of the submarine wreck as a target, the AZORIAN control center crew practiced procedures for the critical maneuvers required for set-down and target capture.

To summarize, the hardware and software system specifications for the data processing system were submitted on the 30th of November, 1971, and approved on the 12th of January, 1972. It took a period of approximately 19 months (23 May 1971 to 2 January 1973) to design, build, and deliver the system. It was delivered to the HGE while she was at the Sun Shipyard in Chester, Pa. The system required only general refurbishment in preparation for the MATADOR program.

Field Engineering:

As engineers know, all the design and laboratory testing in the world can't anticipate each and every problem that will surface when you "go out into the field," since that's where Yankee ingenuity and Kentucky windage come to the fore. AZORIAN was no exception to this general rule. A few examples should make this point. Engineering purists may not approve of all these tactics used, while those with a more practical bent will understand and should find beauty in them.

After the first deployment of the pipe string during an integrated systems test off Catalina Island, some of the threaded joints connecting two pieces of pipe became frozen together, and no amount of applied force from the shipboard detorquing machine could loosen the joints. The immediate problem was to devise a method to unscrew the pieces of pipe without damaging them. Next, the cause of the problem and a solution for it had to be found. A retired Navy engineering officer solved the immediate problem. He quickly designed what was probably the world's largest and strongest spanner wrench. (Figure 29 shows this wrench in action.)

Figure 29. The Super wrench being readied to free a stuck joint.

Made from high-strength steel and operated with a manual hydraulic jack, Super Wrench could deliver one million foot-pounds of force to the pipe joints. This force, plus a judicious heating of the outer surface of the pipe joint, produced the desired effect with no serious damage to the threads.

As for the cause of the problem, it was determined that inadvertently a natural battery had been built into the threaded joint. The surfaces of the threads were coated with zinc and then covered with a normal oil field lubricant to prevent sticking and galling. Red lead was a constituent of the lubricant, and this together with the zinc formed the two opposing plates of a battery.

Figure 30. Examining red lead coated threads for damage.

All that was needed to complete the circuit was an electrical conducting medium to connect the two. Even with tightly threaded pipe joints, enough sea water was forced into the joint to provide the electrical path. The resulting corrosion caused the threads to lock.

Figure 31. Applying Aqua-Lube to the threads. It didn't work and had to be removed.

Immediate testing of alternative lubricants was started. One, a very sticky, gooey synthetic mix called Aqua-Lube proved to have insufficient holding power. The final solution was a blend of titanium dioxide, silicon dioxide, and zinc chromate in a silicone oil.

After testing on the one-eighth scale model pipe, this new lubricant was used successfully on all the joints—but only after each full-scale joint had been thoroughly cleaned of the red lead and Aqua-Lube mixtures, perhaps one of the messiest jobs ever undertaken by mankind (Figure 30 and 31).

Another quite different problem occurred during the operation in which the HGE picked up the capture vehicle from the submerged barge.

In the program jargon this exercise was called mating. Not only was there an engineering mating taking place, but unbeknownst to the ship's crew—there was a biological mating taking place too. The squid had returned to Catalina for their annual frolic in the shallow waters of Isthmus Cove (Figure 32).

Figure 32. The HGE at the mating site at Isthmus Cove, Catalina. She is moored over the submerged barge HMB-1.

After the capture vehicle was securely stowed within the HGE and the well-gates were shut, the pumps started removing the water from the well. This lasted only a short while, since the pumps were constantly becoming clogged up with ecstatic squid, and no headway could be made in removing the water. Eventually the HGE was moved out of the cove into deeper water, the gates were reopened, and lights were hung over the side (it was the middle of the night) to draw the squid out of the well. Luckily the lighting seemed to discourage encounters of the sexual kind, so out came the squid; the gates were re-closed, and the pumps were free of squid except for a few unfortunate stragglers left behind.

One last example from the mission will show still another form of engineering fixes—using a man to replace a device. Two large cylindrical devices called heave compensators absorbed the up-and-down motion of the sea and kept the rig floor (the pipe deployment area) at a constant level. These shock absorbers were located under the rig floor, fore and aft, and had a total stroke length of 14 feet. It was critical that they move in unison, for if they got out of synchronization, the rig floor would become canted, not only causing metal-to-metal contact (and damage) but also putting a severe strain on the deployed pipe string.

Devices called rotapulsers measured the amount of stroke in each of the heave compensator cylinders. The measurement in each rotapulser was made by a wire which was on a pulley and a distance counter. This information was constantly fed to the control center for the lifting operation and was used to automatically keep the two cylinders in synchronization. Various problems had been experienced with the rotapulser, but on one occasion during the mission the wires failed. The cylinders got out of "sync," and the resulting metal-to-metal contact caused an impressive display of sparks and noises, along with real damage. It wasn't a mission-ending failure, but because the operation was in a critical phase, it had to continue while the wires were replaced.

To gather the position information needed to keep the heave compensators in unison, a quite simple method was devised. Yardsticks were affixed to the ship near the moving cylinders and a welding rod was used as an indicator needle. One man with a headset telephone was stationed at each of the cylinders to read out the positions of the rods on the yardsticks as the cylinders moved up and down. The men at the other end of the phone in the heavy lift control center could then control the relative position of the two cylinders. It was a simple but effective solution to a nasty problem.

Later calculations showed that the wires had failed at their predicted life cycle. The number of accumulated cycles on the wires had even exceeded the original predictions—a small fact easily overlooked in the stress of solving the larger and more pressing problems of the day.

The Price Tag:

Various charges about exorbitant cost escalations were levied on the engineering procurement for Project AZORIAN. The most critical one claimed that the Agency sold the program on the basis of an initial estimate. Unfortunately charges such as this one were made without a careful examination of what actually took place, so here is a history of the cost growth with Project AZORIAN:

a. Fall 1969 to Summer 1970:

The original AZORIAN concept used pentane tankage to provide buoyancy for lift, and anticipated a total program encompassing three years. The recovery was to be performed covertly by means of specially constructed salvage barges with the target-lifting barge mated within a larger barge. The target was to be exploited within a safe harbor. No testing costs prior to the mission were included in the preliminary estimate. The earliest cost information included estimates for design work, the barge and for operational costs up to the third year. Barge cost estimates were based on costs per pound for barge construction. Subsequent tank tests showed that interactions between the subsurface and surface salvage barges were impossible to control, and the use of pentane lift under these circumstances was too dangerous. The buoyancy concept was therefore abandoned.

By the Spring of 1970 the complexity and problems associated with the buoyancy concept were more fully understood and a test program had been added. The dollar estimate increased as a result. No attempt had yet been made to get program approval. The barge concept wasn't used but more importantly the program wasn't sold at this time with these early cost estimates. Thus, the claims that cost growth estimates should use this earlier base are erroneous.

b. October 1970 to early 1971:

The initial concept of a system for covertly lifting the target by using heavy lifting equipment mounted aboard a large surface ship was now better developed. Equally important, however, was the development of management and cover concepts using the image of Howard Hughes with the more plausible cover of a commercial deep ocean mining effort.

These initially-estimated costs were based on incomplete data and with a recovery projected for completion in 1973. Estimates were also obtained by scaling up the cost of an existing smaller vessel (the Glomar Challenger).

On the 16th of November, 1970, the procurement of certain long-lead-time equipment was authorized for the first time. Some people, therefore, argue that this current working estimate should be taken as the cost base. Those who would do so should remember that the initiation of procurement of long-lead items doesn't constitute a full program go-ahead.

This type of procurement contract can be stopped with relatively small default penalties. In addition there were still 11 major unknown or technical risk areas facing the engineers at this time. Resolution of these would almost certainly increase the costs.

National-level senior management was advised of these, as was the ExCom. In fact, a five-month hold on major procurements was placed on the program two weeks after authorization for certain long-lead items was obtained.

c. March 1971—July 1971:

During the earlier period, the systems specifications and a total scenario for the project were still under development, but in March of 1971 the first estimates were given to ExCom based on a preliminary design study and, as such, might be considered as a reference point for the base cost on the project.

d. August 1971—March 1972:

Estimates presented at the March of 1971 ExCom meeting had listed a number of uncertainties and costs that further clarification would refine. Based on a year-long detailed computer measurement study of photography, it became apparent that the target was lying more nearly on her side than previously estimated, thereby increasing the effective width of the target.

As described earlier, this required a significant redesign of the surface ship and capture vehicle. An additional cost growth was experienced due to the strengthening of the lift shoulder of the pipe string. These cost increases caused the ExCom, in August of 1971, to undertake a total review of the

AZORIAN project and to order a moratorium on major procurement actions.

The moratorium included deferring the keel laying of the surface ship. After a full review of the target value, program costs, cover and risks, on the 1st of October, 1971, the ExCom decided to proceed with the AZORIAN Project.

There were still a few uncertainties left in the engineering areas: work needed to be done on the control system, including the fail-safe portions of the heavy lift system; the grabber configuration on the CV wasn't finalized, nor were the operator displays, or the breakout legs, or the hydraulic system. The software for the computer system was just starting and simulation studies were still being run to determine operational red-lines for the equipment.

Since ExCom finally decided to proceed with AZORIAN and the keel was laid in November, the dollar estimate given at this time could serve as the cost base.

The keel laying was a most significant event. It would be difficult to explain stopping the ship's construction after this item had occurred, so a cancellation now would be costly in both dollars and a credibility sense.

e. April 1972—July 1972:

Contracts were now made definite with the four prime contractors. The new program increases derived from the funding required for engineering change proposals, proof-test equipment, extra costs associated with the construction barge, and increases to cover the post-acquisition handling.

An argument could be made that the basis for cost growth should be taken from this base, when the contracts were made definite.

At this time a major program review was undertaken by the Special Projects Staff in order to remove any "gold plating" from the hardware or any other aspects of the project.

There was great pressure to make an attempt to keep the total costs under $200 million. At the same time, ExCom again reviewed and approved the continuation of AZORIAN.

f. August 1972—September 1974:

Another increase in costs happened principally by the structural modifications needed to the surface ship's design to meet U.S. Coast Guard specifications, which were a prerequisite to obtaining the needed maritime risk insurance. A furious debate was going on over AZORIAN, with a strong effort being mounted by senior Navy and Defense Department officials to kill the program.

ExCom decided to go to the 40 Committee for a political assessment on running the operation in 1974. The upshot of all this was that President Nixon wrote a letter praising the project and approving its continuation. As a result, all debate on AZORIAN effectively ended.

g. Cost Summary:

There are five points in time during the AZORIAN program that could be used to establish a cost basis on which to calculate cost escalations. Of these five, two are not really valid. The first estimates of late 1969 and early 1970, in fact, are meaningless. They were based on a concept that was never used, and no program approvals or decisions were made on their merit. The charge that AZORIAN was thus sold as a cheaper project is therefore without foundation. The next estimate made in October of 1970 also had little validity. It was made without having preliminary engineering or a total program scenario in hand. No major procurements were authorized; they were in fact expressly forbidden. Limited long-lead procurement was authorized at this time, but it can't be said that a full program approval was obtained. In the view of the project managers, the only valid dates for setting a base cost estimate are for March of 1971 and August of 1971. By March a total scenario had been developed covering all the essential elements of the program and the preliminary engineering had been completed. Although major long-lead procurements had been authorized, the ExCom was aware that significant engineering uncertainties remained and that their resolution could increase the costs. By August most of these solutions had been worked out and their costs estimated; a major one was the required redesigning of the ship's hull. ExCom ordered the keel laying postponed until a thorough review was conducted, but the review was favorable and the keel was laid as planned in November of 1971.

The estimate made in August of 1971, then, is the best point from which to calculate the cost escalation, for it was then that ExCom authorized the keel laying, a momentous undertaking after which it would be difficult to abandon the ship's construction.

HGE Trials And Tests:

The HGE's trials and tests were divided into three separate categories:

1. Ship testing on general items including trim and ballast, dual pilot houses, lifeboat drills, and vibration.
2. Standard ship tests which involved main propulsion, speed trials, turning radius, astern and emergency steering, stabilizing system, calibration of propulsion and thruster motors.
3. Unconventional ship tests such as checking the docking legs, gimbal bearings, and accuracy of the dynamic positioning system.

Summary Of Trials—Builder's Trials:

The HGE left the Sun Shipyard at Chester, Pa., on the 12th of April, 1973, then sailed down the Delaware River and across Delaware Bay, then out into the Atlantic Ocean where all the tests were conducted in an area roughly 75 nautical miles southeast of Delaware Bay. There were 203 various people aboard, either participating in or observing the trials. Sun Shipyard had four key operating personnel with four who were supervising, and also a large number of engineers, electricians, pipe fitters, and operating crew; Global Marine had 58 representatives including an engineering group; and the Special Project Staff had several representatives under cover. The American Bureau of Shipping and the U.S. Coast Guard also had several representatives aboard.

The ship and her equipment were operated by Sun Ship personnel only, and tests and trials were carried out under normal operating conditions, in good weather and calm seas. All scheduled tests were accomplished successfully in all areas. The ship's handling throughout the tests was reported as follows: "HGE's overall seaworthiness, mobility, and response was excellent." A few major and a number of minor discrepancies were noted which Sun Ship and Global Marine were responsible for correcting before the ship was delivered.

Builder's trials were concluded late in the evening on the 14th of April with completion of thruster tests. The HGE then proceeded to Delaware Bay and retraced her route up the Delaware River, arriving at Sun Shipbuilding, Chester, Pa., on the 15th of April. Upon returning to Sun Shipyard, the HGE underwent a major effort to correct any deficiencies and ready herself for delivery to Global Marine as operator for the U.S. Government, with completion of East Coast trials scheduled for early July, 1973.

East Coast Trials, July—August 1973:

Even though all the marine systems were given their first sea test during the builder's trials, it was the intent during East Coast trials to test the most basic marine systems again and to record test data. Furthermore, a great many systems hadn't been tested at sea during the builder's trials and couldn't be adequately tested at the dock, such as heavy lift, docking legs, heave compensator, the gimbal platform, and the pipe-handling system, and test personnel were to give maximum effort to these. Dockside work at Sun Shipbuilding was completed early in July, and the Hughes Glomar Explorer set out for East Coast trials on the 24th of July, 1973. Curtis Crooke of GMI was designated overall test director, and each test was assigned a principal reviewer from the Global Marine review team. As discrepancies were encountered and recorded, reviewers were responsible for signing off formal acceptance or rejection of each test.

Ship's activities were scheduled from departure from the Sun Shipyard dock until her arrival later at Hamilton, Bermuda—the first port of call—including some 47 different tests or activities which were conducted in six main areas.

As the HGE headed south down the Delaware River at low tide, it passed under two bridges and one power line. One bridge was the Delaware Memorial Bridge at Wilmington. To get the ship under the 225-foot-high span, the top 28 feet of the derrick had to be removed and stored on her main deck. Once below the bridge, the Sun 200, a huge floating crane, picked up the 28-foot section and placed it back atop the 200-foot derrick, where it was secured.

After shallow-water tests off of Delaware Bay, the ship proceeded to the deep-water test location 80 miles northwest of Bermuda, where the Automatic Station Keeping (ASK) system had its first test in deep water; about ten double sections (600 feet) of heavy pipe were run in the pipe-handling system; and the gimbal platform was put through its first fully operational test. At the conclusion of test activities, the ship proceeded to Bermuda for a crew change with final preparation and loading for the East-West transit to Long Beach, California, by transiting around South America via the Strait of Magellan.

Results Of East Coast Trials:

It was concluded that except for a few deficiencies, the HGE's basic ship systems had performed very well, and she was capable of completing her intended job. The hull was determined to be sound, with no apparent flaws or weaknesses. Major structural assemblies such as the well-gates, A-frame, gimbal platform, derrick, and docking legs all appeared to be structurally sound with satisfactory alignment and fit, so that no major structural rework or change in concept of the basic systems was required. For the most part, all mining equipment items operated as designed, although there were several serious deficiencies and many minor ones. Corrective work was scheduled to begin during the transit to Long Beach and early on in West Coast mobilization for the mission. To illustrate the complexity and magnitude of readying the ship for West Coast testing, it was determined immediately after East Coast trials that 40 corrective tasks would be performed prior to her departure from Bermuda, 136 tasks would be performed during transit to Long Beach, and 245 tasks would be performed as soon as possible during West Coast mobilization.

East-West Transit, 11 August—30 Sept. 1973:

After completion of her East Coast trials, the Glomar Explorer remained at anchor off Bermuda on the 9th through the 11th of August, 1973, while a crew change was accomplished and all preparations completed for the 12,700-mile voyage to Long Beach. This was planned to take just over 50 days at an average speed of 10.5 knots. The long way around was necessary because the HGE's 116-foot beam was too wide to permit her passage through the Panama Canal. A transit crew of 96 personnel was decided upon, of whom 47 were regular ship's crew and the remaining 49 were Global Marine engineers and technicians who used the time in transit to complete a number of fitting-out tasks.

Arrangements were made through the Global Marine agent in Valparaiso, Chile, to carry two Chilean pilots for the transit through the Strait of Magellan. They were to board the HGE in Possession Bay on the Atlantic side, provide the ship safe passage for the 320 mile journey through the Strait to the Pacific Ocean, and ride the ship to Valparaiso for disembarkation.

The replacement crew for the East-West transit was flown to Bermuda from Los Angeles on the 10th of August, 1973. By midday on the 11th, engine modifications had been completed, stores and provisions loaded, and final preparations completed, so that the ship was underway from the Bermuda anchorage at 1630.

Because the HGE was government property, there was a senior U.S. Government representative onboard as commander—as differentiated from the ship's captain. The commander's responsibility was to ensure that the government's best interests were served even though the ship was in a "white"—i.e., commercial configuration, and the majority of the crew weren't knowledgeable about the AZORIAN program. U.S. Government representatives used aliases as they were under tight security cover for the voyage. The HGE's captain and a few others were briefed and aware of proper actions to take in the event of a political incident en route to Long Beach.

Bermuda To Magellan Strait, 11 August— 5 Sept. 1973:

Weather was consistently excellent throughout this leg, although 50 to 60-knot winds and 15 to 20-foot seas were experienced for a brief period while passing through a storm front.

The HGE handled and rode well; a work routine was established, and good progress was made on all transit tasks; morale was good, and the marine crew was competent and well organized. Morale was helped by a well-staffed galley (three cooks and two bakers) which produced superb food for everyone.

During the latter part of August, news reports from Chile verified that the Allende government was experiencing problems, with the possibility of some widespread labor strikes. Although it was considered unlikely, project headquarters developed plans for the possibility that Chilean pilots might not be available for the passage through the Strait of Magellan.

Additionally, contingency plans were prepared in the event Chilean or Argentine ships showed intentions of interfering with the HGE. Alternative options were prepared in case passage through the Strait was denied or it was deemed politically inadvisable to go through. These options were: (1) standing off the coast of South America until things settled down, (2) going around Cape Horn into the Pacific, or (3) going east around South Africa, through the Indian Ocean, then through to the Pacific. As events turned out, an alternative path wasn't required.

Magellan Strait, 5–6 Sept. 1973:

The HGE arrived at the entrance to the Strait on the 5th of September and anchored in Possession Bay, then the two

Chilean pilots came aboard at 1100 local time. The transit was made without incident, although during the latter half of the passage the ship went through a cold front with accompanying winds of 45 to 50 knots. This slowed her progress somewhat, but the HGE cleared the Strait of Magellan and entered the Pacific Ocean at approximately 1500 on the 6th of September. (Figure 33.)

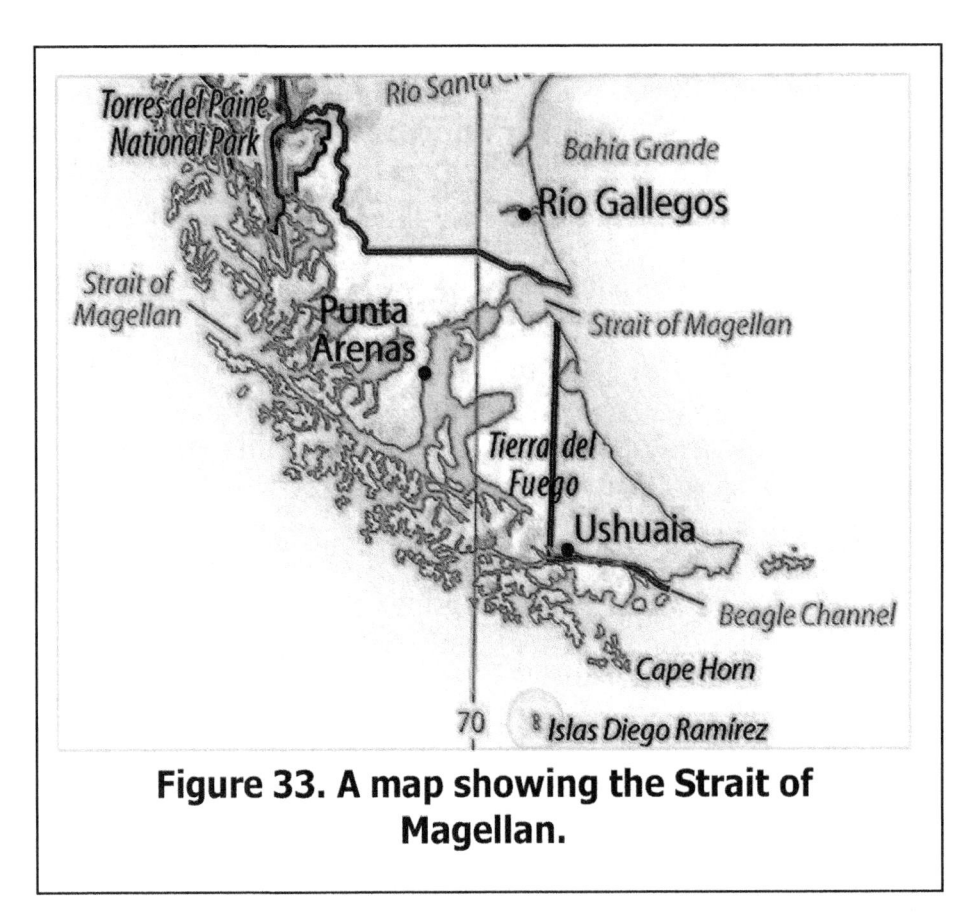

Figure 33. A map showing the Strait of Magellan.

Magellan to Valparaiso, 6-13 Sept. 1973:

Immediately after entering the Pacific Ocean, the HGE ran into extremely heavy weather which slowed her progress again, and actually forced the ship to heave to for a short period in 60-knot winds and 25-foot seas. Throughout these conditions, however, the ship handled beautifully, rode well, and her performance was never a concern to the crew.

The remainder of the leg into Valparaiso, Chile was uneventful, and the ship's crew used this time to complete their list of parts and supplies to be loaded at Valparaiso when the pilots were disembarked. During the few days preceding an 11th of September military coup, the ship's commander monitored commercial radio broadcasts as the HGE approached Valparaiso, and he was aware of the increasing tensions developing in both Santiago and Valparaiso. Nevertheless, he and the HGE's captain, Louis Kingma, didn't allow any concerns over these events to show in their daily messages back to headquarters.

The HGE anchored in the outer harbor of Valparaiso at 2100 local time on the 12th of September. Shortly after her arrival, a small Chilean naval launch came alongside, and a naval officer and seaman came aboard for discussions with Captain Kingma, at which time the ship was formally entered into the port where Kingma was apprised of the military coup in Chile. Because a curfew was in effect, no further personnel movements to the ship could be accomplished that night, but the two Chilean pilots left the HGE with the Chilean naval personnel.

Back on the 7th of September, prior to these events, Global Marine's enterprising personnel representative had left Los Angeles for Santiago, accompanied by one other Global Marine employee. They'd brought with them some 28 boxes of materials and supplies for the HGE, as well as a bag of personal mail. Their principal task was to arrange for the transfer of the supplies and, more importantly, enable the entry into Chile of seven technicians with their transfer to the HGE, all of this having been programmed in early August. They arrived in Santiago on the 8th of September, and with the assistance of other representatives, processed the supplies through customs and proceeded to Valparaiso.

On Monday, the 10th of September, Global Marine's representatives traveled to Santiago again to meet with six personnel who, along with their tools, luggage, and supplies, were all processed and cleared by Customs. The entire party then returned to Valparaiso and settled in the Hotel O'Higgins to await the arrival of the HGE on the 12th of September.

At approximately 0600 on the 11th of September, the Americans were awakened by some loud noises outside their hotel. It was evident the revolution had started, as there were soldiers, tanks, armored cars, and other military vehicles all over the city. The hotel was surrounded, communications had been cut off, and guests were confined to the hotel for the next two to three days.

As attested to in his trip report—which reads like a Hollywood script—Tom Williams, the GMI personnel representative, encountered much intrigue and suspense in getting the seven technicians, supplies, and parts loaded aboard the HGE in the midst of the revolution. Nevertheless, in spite of a curfew, lack of communications, and the general confusion, Williams did a magnificent job of getting to the right people in the new government so that at approximately noon on the 13th of September, all persons and supplies were allowed aboard the HGE, and the ship was cleared to leave Valparaiso.

The HGE weighed anchor at 1500 and sailed for Long Beach. The presence of a covert U.S. intelligence ship in a Chilean port during the military coup was a bizarre coincidence quite unrelated to the rumors that "the CIA had 200 agents in Chile for the sole purpose of ousting Allende." Just as importantly, there were no unfavorable incidents involving the ship, any crew members, or the Global Marine representative throughout this time.

Valparaiso To Long Beach, CA, 13-30 Sept. 1973:

This leg of the voyage was completed without incident. The weather was excellent with the exception of two tropical storms that the ship easily avoided; work progressed well, and the HGE made a final report on her transit task completions. Only 21 scheduled jobs weren't completed due to time constraints. The heavy-lift team which had boarded at Valparaiso made excellent progress, following a preplanned work schedule. The HGE arrived in Long Beach at 1700 PST, on the 30th of September, and tied up at Pier E without incident. As it was a Sunday evening, the ship's arrival didn't attract undue attention; stores were loaded and the relief crew came aboard early Monday to conclude the East-West transit phase of the AZORIAN program.

During her transit from the Atlantic to the Pacific, the HGE traveled 12,745 nm in 50 days, 7 hours and 30 minutes, for an average speed of 10.8 knots. A total of 20,643 barrels of fuel were consumed, which equates to 68 gallons per mile.

Mobilization For Mission, Oct. 1973—January 1974:

After the East-West transit and arrival at Long Beach on the 30th of September, the HGE began a period of mobilization for the mission that would end with some further systems testing. While this final "fitting out" period was originally allocated approximately 51 days to complete, it would actually take about twice that long, with the primary purpose of in-port mobilization to convert the ship from an overt into a covert configuration. During this same time, operations personnel activated the mission team and began an intensive training program which was accomplished aboard the ship as vans and equipment were installed, checked out, and made available to users.

After a considerable discussion and analysis of the number of crew members required for the mission, a total of 178 individuals were scheduled—the maximum amount possible limited by lifeboat capacity. Despite distractions such as the busy pier-side maintenance activity in the area, the crew members, ship workers, and technicians turned to their specialized assignments with a high degree of technical competence, motivation, and morale. The mobilization period produced a cohesive team effort for the mission, and presented the first opportunity to assemble a mission team in accordance with key functions and positions established earlier in the program. Key mission personnel were: Mission Director, Deputy Mission Director, Deputy for Recovery, Deputy for Handling, Deputy for Exploitation, Deputy for Operations; Director, Technical Staff, and Ship's Captain. Although the ship's captain normally takes command of a vessel, the Mission Director was the senior command authority aboard the Glomar Explorer because of the unique mission and responsibility required for the operation of the complete AZORIAN recovery system. At sea, he alone was responsible for the implementation of contingency or emergency plans, if required, while maintaining the overall mission security and cover. As an indication of the thoroughness of pre-mission planning, when the HGE sailed on the recovery mission in June of 1974, the shipboard mission team and organization were surprisingly very similar to what was originally set down on paper back in 1971 and 1972.

Mission Financing:

*A*nd *how was this whole thing financed? According to a Soviet investigation, it was postulated the entire operation cost around $350 millions dollars, and was funded through Howard Hughes.*

However, a possibility popped up that the CIA secretly was involved in the recovery of gold from a 17th century sunken galleon found off the southern California Coastal area. This recovery was done later by the Glomar Explorer near Catalina Island in 1975. A lawsuit was filed by the original finders of the shipwreck, but it ended up dismissed with no apparent explanation.

Of particular note is the three people who knew the most about this whole operation from the United States point of view eventually departed for various reasons: Richard Nixon resigned as President, CIA Director Colby was replaced, and Howard Hughes died from something he was most scared of while living within a sterile environment—flu bugs.

The CIA started picking the crew for this dangerous mission prior to the ship's completion, with enough time to train them in the necessary skills required for a recovery. They preferred to get sailors that came out of the Navy and were familiar with submarines, and also were able to keep something a secret.

After certain selections, classes were held to educate the crew about their tasks ahead. But the content was somewhat strange: they needed to learn Russian terms that translated into Code Room, Caution: Radiation, Control Room, etc. and were also taught to understand everything about measuring radiation and identifying diesel submarine parts. Since they were given no prior knowledge of where they were going or for what reason, all they could do was think of the possibilities.

At least until a few days prior to the ship's departure, where they were informed of the planned mission. They were also told about the many dangers involved, including the possibility of being taken prisoner should the Soviet Union find out and board the ship.

The submarine they were to raise contained nuclear warheads, and had sunk at great depths. Naturally there *would be dead bodies involved, just as they were trained in how to handle such matters. Then when asked if they all still wanted to take part in the mission, only one person declined.*

Conversion Of The HGE From "White" To "Black"

From July of 1973 when the HGE left Sun Shipyard in Chester, Pa., through the east coast trials and the transit from the east coast around South America to the west coast, the ship was in a completely "white" configuration. That is, there was no equipment or activity aboard which would indicate her intelligence nature or the projected recovery operation. Although the HGE had some unique features such as the massive "A" frame, the unusually large well area, and the towering derrick (236 feet above the waterline), all these items could be attributed to a prototype mining vessel which required them for the heretofore unexplored mission of deep-ocean mining.

During mobilization, the primary effort was to install equipment and facilities for the recovery mission and for the exploitation of all the the valuable intelligence items expected to be found. Twenty-four mission vans were loaded and installed aboard ship for these purposes. They had been prefabricated into a standard 8 foot x 8 foot x 20 foot size and delivered to contractors for outfitting with specialized mission gear. For example, 20 such vans were equipped and then trucked to Long Beach for loading aboard the ship under tight security.

All ship-to-shore communications were open and transmitted via commercial radio circuits using radio teletype or manual Morse code. Commercial messages were addressed to Global Marine, Inc., Los Angeles, and were normally handled by RCA radio station KPH in San Francisco. Weather observations were transmitted to Coast

Guard stations for further relay to Fleet Numerical Weather Central. Global Marine responded to the ship's messages as required by answering these in a normal commercial manner via the normal commercial radio circuits. These messages to the ship helped to maintain the appearance that Global Marine was controlling all the operations concerning the HGE.

Onboard there were two control vans that served as the nerve center of operations. Other vans were installed in appropriate positions on the HGE for such purposes as:

1. Cleaning: a facility fitted out for the ultrasonic cleaning and preservation of any items recovered from the submarine.

2. Decontamination: separate rooms for decontaminating exploitation personnel and to target materials containing nuclear contaminants.

3. Paper processing: a facility for processing and restoring the great volume of manuals, documents, and other printed material expected from the target.

4. Drying: a special facility for the proper drying of documents and other items.

5. Darkroom: a facility to process the large amount of photographs taken to record any recovered intelligence material.

6. Waste handling: used to safeguard and handle any nuclear-contaminated materials.

7. Dress out and change rooms: various facilities for personnel working in the well to change and clean up after any exposure to possible nuclear contamination.

8. Packing: a facility for wrapping and crating recovered items for shipment to exploitation facilities within the United States.

Weather Facilities:

Meteorologists were assigned to provide onboard meteorological and oceanographic expertise which was imperative to the mission. The aft chart room, adjacent to the aft bridge and pilot house, housed the meteorology office, display center, and a main weather equipment space. The HGE's shipboard capability for reception of weather data included all the required advanced equipment necessary for the mission.

Manning:

As in-port mobilization in Long Beach continued, labor-management problems were developing between the Marine Engineers Beneficial Association (MEBA) and Global Marine. As a result, MEBA set up picket lines in an attempt to boycott the Hughes Glomar Explorer at Pier E. This unfortunate situation took a serious turn on the 12th of November, when MEBA escalated its activity from a small group into a mass picketing with about 100 persons participating, including strong-arm types. The resulting tense situation continued for the next week to ten days. During this time, the ship's crew and shipboard workers were harassed, delivery trucks were stopped, and special security measures had to be put into place. This union problem and certain engineering problems made havoc of the mobilization schedule, and with the Christmas-New Year holiday fast approaching, the departure for sea trials became set back until mid-January of 1974.

One of the prerequisites for beginning sea trials was a valid pipe-handling system (PHS) demonstration at dockside. However, on the 9th of January there were still several engineering tasks to be accomplished before the heavy-lift pipe could be moved through the system. It was decided to move the ship from the dock out to the Long Beach outer anchorage and conduct the PHS demonstration there, and then move out for sea trials. The main reasons were the sagging morale of the sea trials crew and the fear that the repeated delays would begin to adversely affect the mission crew's performance. Therefore, rather than risk this, it was decided to give everyone a "shot-in-the-arm" with the move to the outer anchorage.

Because of the delays in getting ready for the sea trials, time was now getting very precious. It was essential that all the tests be completed, the ship be readied for the mission, and she depart to be on station at the target area in early July, since the mission could only be accomplished within the July to mid-September weather window. Only during this period could one expect moderately good weather to last long enough for the operation to be completed. For planning purposes, 14 to 21 days were expected to be required for this recovery sequence. If the HGE couldn't be ready to leave port by mid to late June, the recovery attempt would have to be delayed for a full year.

During the period when the HGE was being mobilized at Pier E (and where she was berthed after the mission as well), Soviet merchant ships usually made routine port calls to Long Beach consisting of two to three days duration. In almost all cases the Soviet ships were docked at Berth 10, located some 400 yards across the channel off the HGE's starboard quarter. Even though the Soviet ships were close to the HGE and had the opportunity for a close inspection, there was no evidence that the Soviets gained any prior knowledge of her true mission, a tribute to the security precautions and mining cover engaged by the ship's crew during the West Coast mobilization.

1st West Coast Trials, 11 January—23 January 1974:

West Coast trials began on the 11th of January when the Glomar Explorer left Pier E at 1230 Pacific time. The MEBA union problems were still plaguing Global Marine, and two union picket boats were present, but neither tried to interfere with the ship. The site for trials was approximately 160 miles west-southwest of Long Beach, where the water depth was expected to be about 12,500 feet. The primary purpose of the test was to verify readiness of the pipe-handling system (PHS) and heavy-lift system (HLS), as well as the readiness of all operating personnel.

The sea trials also would include checks on engine propulsion, navigation systems, and other ship's systems while underway to and from the test site. Upon completion of the tests, the well-gates would be closed and the ship would proceed on approximately the 1st of February to Isthmus Cove at Catalina Island where the HMB-1 would be anchored.

1st Trials Chronology:

After the HGE moved to the outer harbor anchorage, the mining crew ran a double of pipe—60 feet—through the system two or three times; the well was flooded and the PHS and docking legs checked for reliability. After five days at the anchorage, during which a myriad of problems occurred in the PHS, it was concluded that the system had limited reliability in its current configuration. If time hadn't been so critical, the obvious course of action was to return to Pier E for the needed modifications, but all believed that the time lost would be unacceptable since the 1974 weather window would be missed. Even though it became clear that the PHS couldn't be qualified during the trials, it was decided that many priority tests could be completed.

The ship arrived on site at approximately midnight on the 19th of January and deployed long and short baseline transponders on the seafloor as well as the wave-rider buoy, the latter a device which measured, recorded, and continuously transmitted sea-state data to the ship.

On the 21st and 22nd of January, the unfavorable sea state and winds on site delayed the tests, including the important initial step of flooding the well and opening the well-gates. Weather improved temporarily on the 22nd sufficiently, however, so that a supervisor was able to make a quick visit to the ship by helicopter for a first-hand review of test operations.

On the 23rd of January after the well had been flooded, the well-gate opening was in progress when the ship suffered damage in the aft gate operating machinery. The casualty occurred during heavy surges of the sea within the well. An inspection revealed damage to the aft gate seal, distortion to some aft gate drive gear teeth, and damage to the pedestal supporting the aft gear driveshaft. The after well-gate had to be hauled to a closed position by rigging cables and using winches. Because of these problems, it wasn't possible to continue the sea trials. Headquarters was advised that the HGE would return to her Long Beach anchorage for further inspection and repairs. The trip back was uneventful, and time was spent in communications between the ship and Global Marine for ordering parts and technical help for repairs. The HGE arrived at Long Beach harbor on the 24th of January.

Examination of the well-gate damage caused personnel to conclude that although the sea state may have been within the upper limits of the stated specifications for opening the gates, it nevertheless stressed the system too greatly and caused the failure. After a thorough evaluation, engineers estimated 13 to 15 days would be needed to accomplish repairs. With this delay added to the several other major component tasks, it was estimated that everything would be ready for sea again about the 14th of February to complete the West Coast trials.

The repairs had to be accomplished under difficult conditions because there wasn't enough time to move the ship to a drydock large enough to handle her—even if one was immediately available. Thus inspection and some seal repairs instead had to be done by divers. One small but persistent seal leak was never corrected, and the seepage of a few gallons per hour was deemed acceptable. Thus the

Glomar Explorer lived on with a small puddle always in her starboard wing well.

Interestingly, the press took note of the HMB-1 departure from Redwood City in an Associated Press article datelined Redwood City which appeared in the Long Beach Independent Press Telegram. Basically, the article enhanced program cover in that it discussed the barge's connection with the HGE and its role in the Hughes ocean mining venture.

After the safe arrival and mooring of both barges at Catalina, they went into a "sit and wait" mode until the current ship repairs were finished.

2nd West Coast Trials, 15 February—2 March 1974:

Next a selection was made on who would become the Mission Director for all of HGE's operations, and he was an excellent choice, as future events would verify. Not only did he provide the leadership required for this complex and dangerous mission, but his earlier role in preparing to handle the nuclear materials and contaminated items gave the mission crew confidence in an area of little understood danger.

Excellent progress was being made during the in-port work period after the well-gate casualty on the 23rd of January, and it was possible this time to conduct tests immediately upon completion of all repairs and modifications. These included flooding the well and opening the well-gates to check the previously damaged gate drive system. Also, because the well-gates were open, pipe was run through the entire system. All operations were performed satisfactorily to the degree that senior officials considered the ship ready to go back to complete her trials at sea.

GMI Vice President Curtis Crooke was aboard for the new trials as the senior Global Marine official. This position conformed with what the ocean mining world would expect was necessary, since completing trials was a Global Marine contractual responsibility to the U.S. Government.

Performance Criteria For West Coast Trials:

In view of the poor performance and problems with the pipe-handling system during the East Coast and West Coast trials, important specific performance criteria were now established for the PHS and the heavy-lift system for the new trials. These included a reliability demonstration by lowering and raising 60 to 70 doubles of pipe (3,600 to 4,200 feet) with the exact number based on available water depth near Catalina Island. In the event that bad weather or time constraints precluded selection of a site to complete the 60 to 70 doubles requirement, the Mission Director was authorized to allow a moderate back-off from that specific range of pipe lengths. The basic criterion was a "reasonably reliable demonstration," with the sole judge of acceptability and suitability in meeting the test objective.

For the next ten days at the test location, everything and everybody were devoted to solving testing problems, and virtually all tests were successfully completed within the scheduled time frame. Of the problems that surfaced, perhaps the most serious were the malfunctions in the heavy-lift system sensors and controls, which were repaired. More importantly, the pipe-handling system operated satisfactorily with only a few minor delays. A total of 40 doubles of pipe were deployed and recovered (equivalent to 2,400 feet), with the only problem being the untorquing of some joints. All agenda events for trials were satisfactorily completed by the evening of the 25th of February. With an excellent weather outlook projected for Catalina for the next few days, the HGE estimated her arrival at Isthmus Cove at 0700 on the 26 of February.

From Isthmus Cove the Glomar Explorer proceeded to a point 65 nautical miles southwest of Catalina Island to coordinates 32-44N; 119-14W. The technical purpose was to complete roll stabilization tests, but a more compelling reason for leaving the coastal waters was that commercial vessels in California waters on the 1st of March were subject to a special California inventory tax. Rather than face possible scrutiny over the tax which potentially reveals the true ownership of the ship by the U.S. Government, it was decided to be in international waters at that time. After completing tests in the vicinity, the HGE sent a message to that effect and then returned to Long Beach, where she arrived at Pier E at 1645 local time on the 2nd of March. The HGE was scheduled to remain in port for a 25 to 30-day period while finishing the last mobilization tasks still needing completion.

Integrated Systems Tests, 28 March—13 May 1974:

After the ship's return to Pier E at Long Beach on the 2nd of March, the next 25 days were devoted to final preparations on the complete AZORIAN system for the Integrated Systems tests (IST) scheduled to begin on the 28th of March.

Other work on the ship's systems also was being accomplished concurrently at a feverish pace, with particular attention to the pipe string, thread compound, gimbal platform, A-frame, yokes, hydraulic pumps and controls, and docking legs—all considered essential to pipe-handling and heavy-lift systems. Excellent progress was made in all areas. In many cases round-the-clock activity was required to complete these tasks on schedule.

The time pressure of meeting the July to August weather window forced a drastic change in the Integrated Systems tests. An intermediate water depth (about 2,600 feet) site was chosen off Catalina Island where the water was deep enough to exercise the pipe-handling system thoroughly. The HGE left Pier E on schedule at 0045 on the 28th of March, and after mooring at the initial test site eight miles east on the lee side of Catalina Island, they immediately began this test schedule.

Unfortunately a torquer casualty was followed by a minor series of bridle, heavy-lift, and pipe-handling problems which required in-port repairs. Meanwhile, valuable training was accomplished by the Control Center crew, with their personnel performance being outstanding and representing a shot-in-the-arm for crew morale. In view of the many setbacks and delays in the program thus far, it was indeed heartening to know that the overall system was considered operational and had demonstrated satisfactory reliability. The problems and delays encountered previously, however, now required major revisions of the remaining test schedule and scenario. If the recovery mission was to be accomplished in the summer of 1974, a major decision was required now as to the need for further testing versus declaring the system "ready for recovery operations."

Therefore in conjunction with senior CIA officials, it was decided that completion of the system testing at the 2,400-foot depth location would satisfy the requirements for a satisfactory demonstration of system reliability, and that planning would continue for a June departure on the recovery mission. This decision effectively waived the need for a deep test to 12,000 feet. A major factor in this decision was confidence in the recovery crew performance. Additionally, what had been an earlier recognition of two factors was coming into a renewed and clearer focus. The first was that this unique recovery system was unparalleled in size and complexity and the first ever to operate at these depths and loads. The second was that the system design was based upon a one-time operation, not a series of repetitive tests and development operations such as with a new airplane. Further testing would create additional confidence, but would also place further wear and tear on the system.

AZORIAN was the world's largest salvage operation, and its success after preliminary test demonstrations would depend upon the crew and their ability to devise "work-arounds" for the many problems which would never go away completely—no matter how many tests were conducted. These risks were inherent and some would remain, no matter what. Furthermore, no testing (short of the mission itself) could ever duplicate the target, with its unknowns of structural integrity, stability, and breakout characteristics.

As planned just before completion of the Integrated Systems tests at sea, elements of the underwater teams directed by the Deputy for Handling and Deputy for Exploitation were put aboard the HGE to familiarize themselves with their work areas, equipment, and procedures in the at-sea atmosphere.

On the 12th of May, 1974, the ship advised project headquarters that all the scheduled tests were finally completed. The gates were closed, the well pumped down, and the HGE returned to Long Beach. She moored in the early morning hours on the 13th of May alongside Pier E, where she was scheduled to remain for a 28 to 30-day refitting period in preparation for departure on the recovery mission in mid-June.

An Unusual Note:

*M*ost *days at embassies can be rather mundane, with little happening other than routine work. However during the night-time someone slipped an anonymous note under the door at our Soviet embassy in Washington, D.C., claiming a sunken submarine was to be raised in the Pacific Ocean. It was signed—From a Well Wisher. This information was transmitted by the Soviet ambassador to Moscow and eventually went through the chain to the Pacific Fleet HQ.*

Security Operations:

D-Day for the mission was now approaching rapidly. The Headquarters and office members of security were working on the security annexes to the mission plans: all contingency situations had security connotations. There were casualty and accident plans to be drawn up. How was the port call to be handled? How was the crew change going to be conducted at either Midway or Hawaii? Security strategies and procedures for these situations were formed and incorporated into the mission plans. Wives of the government employees going on the mission were given limited briefings concerning the absence of their husbands. Security officers were to be their point of contact if any of them had problems that they couldn't cope with. There was a flurry of last-minute activity which assured that mission readiness was achieved.

The mission director adopted the program manager's philosophy about the role of security in the program. Onboard the Glomar Explorer, the security officer was part and parcel of all management discussions, and no actions were planned without seeking this security officer's advice and counsel. In this way potential security problems were exposed and resolved before they became flaps.

Final Approval In Washington:

In Washington, the U.S. Intelligence Board's ad hoc committee in April and May of 1974 had made one more evaluation of the expected intelligence benefits of AZORIAN at the request of Dr. Kissinger to support the 40 Committee's discussions regarding approval for the mission to begin in June. This study, approved by USIB in executive session on the 7th of May, was forwarded to Kissinger with a covering memorandum which stated:

"The United States Intelligence Board has reviewed and updated its intelligence assessment of Project AZORIAN. On the basis of this review, the Board concludes that there haven't been any significant developments since the last Board assessment which would detract from the unique intelligence value of this target."

"Acquisition of the nuclear warheads and the SS-N-5 missile system, together with related documents, would provide a much improved baseline for estimates of the current and future Soviet strategic threat. The Board also expects that recovered documents would provide important insights into the Soviet command and control including certain aspects of their strategic attack doctrine."

"In its evaluation the Board assumed a successful mission. On this basis the Board continues to believe that the recovery of the AZORIAN submarine would provide information which can be obtained from no other source, on subjects of great importance to the national defense."

With the planned mission departure date barely a fortnight away, the 40 Committee met to consider AZORIAN on the 5th of June, and Dr. Kissinger prepared a memorandum for the President covering the essential points of the discussion. President Nixon approved the mission on the 7th of June, with the provision that an actual recovery must not be undertaken before his return from an impending 27th of June to 3rd of July visit to the Soviet Union.

Summa Robbery:

With the mission nearly underway, Headquarters security personnel became caught up in the damage assessment of the robbery at the Romaine Street offices of the Summa Corporation. Eventually they had to call in the FBI, which in turn enlisted the Los Angeles Police Department in an attempt to get back an AZORIAN-related document that supposedly was obtained in the burglary. The document never came to light, but the Romaine Street robbery, and the LAPD's attempts to retrieve the document ultimately resulted in the Los Angeles Times story that broke the program's cover during the following year.

AZORIAN Mission, 20 June—13 July 1974:

On the 20th of June, 1974, the HGE moved from her anchorage off of Long Beach to a pre-arranged point outside the three-mile limit for the ceremony to mark Summa's acceptance of the ship, and the next day representatives of Summa and Global Marine arrived by helicopter for the ceremony. They were given a tour of the HGE, including demonstrations in the control center using the lift and other features of the ship. The acceptance ceremony was duly recorded and photographed for cover purposes, after which the representatives returned to Long Beach by way of helicopter.

Later that same day, the HGE set her course for the northwest Pacific and the recovery mission. As the message that day from the HGE to project headquarters indicated, morale was high and preparations for departure had proceeded smoothly.

One crew member recalled the voyage from here: "The sky was leaden, yet the crew had spirits that were as bright as polished silver. Under way at last! Finally, we were really going to do it. The course was set West-Northwest—a direct line to the target. If we could only be there tomorrow—but an eight-knot rate of advance meant a 13-day voyage instead. We wouldn't arrive until the Fourth of July. Surely that would void any evil spirits lurking in a 13-day voyage. But thoughts of any jinxes were in few people's minds. We could do anything. Let Headquarters give us a last-minute change of targets—with this crew and this beautiful ship, no task was too difficult. Mission impossible? Nonsense! "Impossible" wasn't in our vocabulary. Moments like this must contain the true meaning of team spirit, that extra ingredient that hardware will never possess. To experience it once is enough for a career."

On the 27th and 28th of June, several ships passed the HGE on an easterly course, but got no closer than 2 1/2 miles. On the 29th of June, the HGE had already covered a distance of 1,888 miles without incident, and still had 1,120 miles to go. A container ship, Oriental Charge, passed the HGE that day on the port side at a distance of about two miles.

On the 30th of June, various drills were held aboard ship. The Deputy for Exploitation conducted a drill for the control and flow of personnel in and out of the well in the event of a nuclear contamination, the Deputy for Recovery conducted target acquisition dry-runs, and there was also an emergency drill for the destruction of classified documents and equipment. Transit to the recovery site in the Pacific Ocean proceeded further without incident, and on the 4th of July, Independence Day, the HGE arrived at the recovery site at 1301 local time. (President Nixon had already left Moscow the preceding day.) Transponder deployment went relatively smoothly, but several unsatisfactory units had to be rejected before the crew eventually got the six-transponder grid deployed. These were necessary for a precise location of the ship and automatic station-keeping at the recovery site. (Figure 34.)

On the 5th of July, a final and complete analysis was carried out. Two wave-rider buoys were also deployed, and the automatic station-keeping system was calibrated. On the 8th of July, the well-gates were opened.

On the 10th of July, a heavy fog which was present still persisted in the area. After conducting a thorough workout of the pipe-handling system (30 doubles or 1,800 feet of pipe, up and down), this was all completed in only 8 hours. Undocking was delayed, however, because of concerns for the weather. A typhoon was expected to affect the recovery site, and it was decided to sit out the expected high waves.

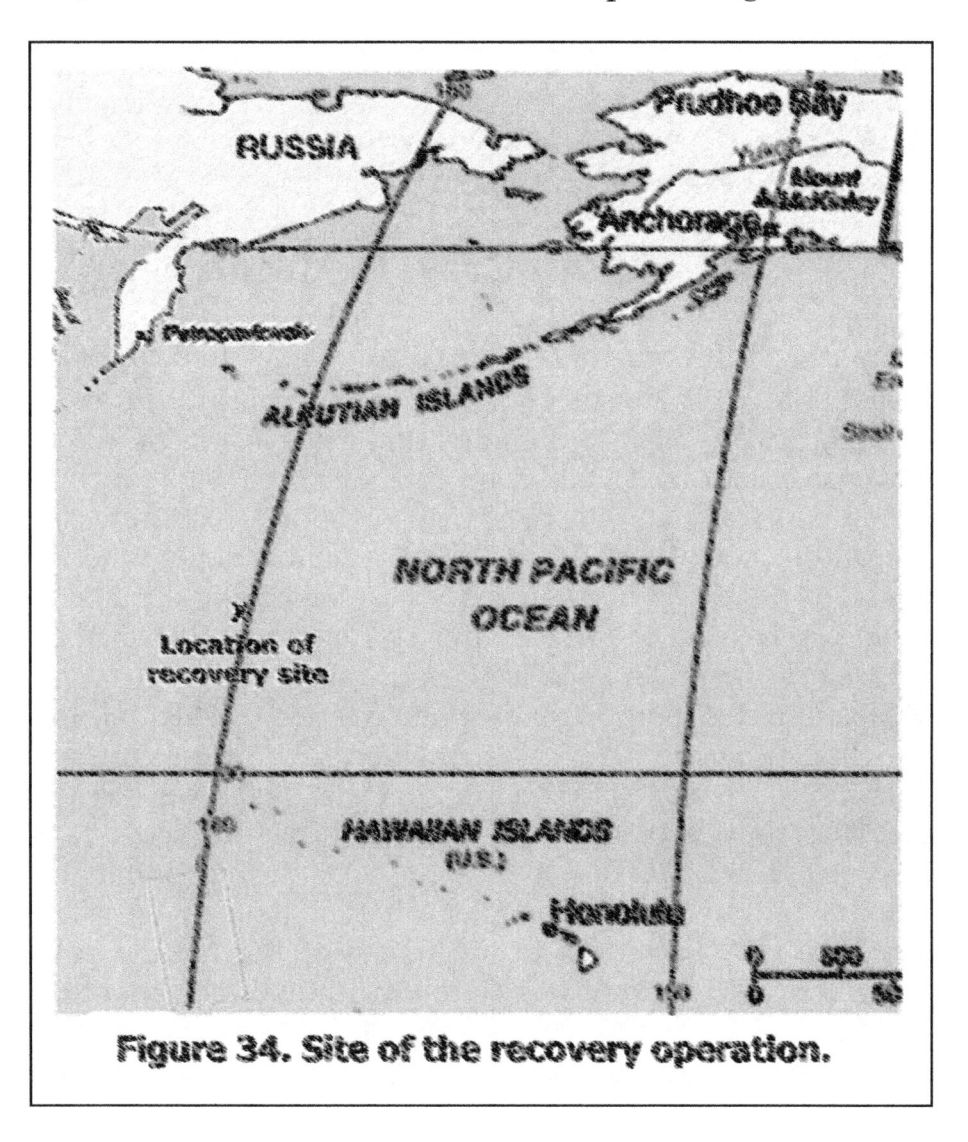

Figure 34. Site of the recovery operation.

On the 11th of July, with waves cresting about 7 feet high, there was a significant vertical surge of water in the well with peaks of about 8 feet, making operations, including camera rigging, very difficult.

The HGE encountered its worst effects from "Gilda" on the 12th of July when a series of long swells (with 15 to 16 seconds of duration between them) came through the area about noon with a combined significant height of 9 to 10 feet, and going as high as 22 feet. However the crisis seemed to be over by the 13th of July, as the waves had already subsided to peaking at only 8 to 9 feet in height.

A Stricken Crew Member:

Observing it was customary for ships with doctors aboard to respond to calls for medical help from nearby vessels, it occurred to the security planners that a suspicious or merely curious captain could fake a medical emergency to get some of his personnel aboard the Hughes Glomar Explorer. And indeed on the 13th of July a British freighter named the Bel Hudson—which earlier had requested medical assistance by radio—arrived on the scene after stating a member of their crew had suffered an apparent heart attack.

Headquarters contingency planning for AZORIAN had anticipated such an event, however, and a pre-mission decision was made based on humanitarian and cover reasons that the crew would respond to medical emergencies if possible. Nevertheless, it was important to ponder the situation carefully and consider whether it might be some sort of a ploy based on an awareness of the mission, and make certain that there wasn't an unwitting disclosure of the HGE's activities. The HGE's surgeon, accompanied by a medical technician and a security officer, along with a British boatswain, made the precarious trip over to the Bel Hudson to examine the patient. After diagnosing the patient and determining he hadn't had a heart attack (as the Bel Hudson had earlier described the ailment) the doctor brought the patient back to the HGE for X-rays and treatment. He relieved the patient's severe internal discomfort and returned him to the Bel Hudson aboard one of their lifeboats. The security officer was also satisfied that the British captain's request was legitimate and that no penetration effort had been attempted.

Throughout the incident, careful security precautions were taken so no mission activities were exposed. The captain of the Bel Hudson was very grateful to the HGE and to the doctor in particular, for his assistance and skillful diagnosis and treatment which quickly improved the seaman's condition. The incident ultimately worked to the advantage of the HGE as far as cover was concerned. As the Bel Hudson and the HGE were arranging the rendezvous position, the British ship had asked, via the open radio circuit, what activities the HGE was engaging in. The HGE responded that it was performing deep-ocean mining testing using a prototype mining machine. It was hoped that the Soviets were monitoring this exchange.

AZORIAN Mission, 14 July—18 July 1974:

By the 14th of July the weather had subsided enough for the crew to consider undocking procedures, although higher seas were predicted for the 15th. On the evening of the 14th, unfortunately, cracks were discovered in the forward port and after starboard docking leg guide structures and were considered a serious problem and difficult to repair. With the weather uncertain, there was concern whether the cracks could be repaired properly before further damage might result, which could cause an aborting of the mission. The ship's heading was adjusted and canvas screens rigged to provide as much protection as possible for the critical welding repair job, which took the next 72 hours to complete. Then the weather took a turn for the worse as tropical storm "Harriet" was causing high seas, and the Mission Team became reluctant to risk any lives for this. So for safety reasons, a decision was made to close the well-gates, and be prepared to leave the recovery site if the wave conditions became too extreme. The well-gates were closed on the 16th of July amid 6-foot waves with no big problems being encountered, but closing the huge well-gates was never a dull exercise aboard the HGE.

The security officer worked with the ship's crew to be sure that the well area was secure from visual observation, as well as Soviet satellite surveillance. In his work with the crew, the security officer also became the crew's morale officer. His success in generating crew support and confidence was a very positive factor in keeping the crew together during the periods of Soviet surveillance and later on when the news media were on to the program.

The weather hold continued on the 17th of July when the HGE was advised about a Soviet naval ship, the Missile Range Instrumentation Ship Chazhma, being underway on a course towards the recovery site and was expected in the immediate vicinity of the HGE at 0400 hours on the 18th. The Chazhma, at 459 feet long, carried a helicopter and was based in Petropavlovsk. As a precaution, the Mission Director ordered that piles of canvas-covered crates be placed on the HGE's helicopter deck to preclude the possibility that the Soviet helicopter might land on the HGE for any reason. Chazhma had originally sailed from Petropavlovsk on the 15th of June to support a SOYUZ/SALYUT space event, and during the 10th to the 13th of July began her return trip to Petropavlovsk from the Johnston Island area. During the early morning hours, the bridge was reporting foggy conditions as patchy and visibility of less than five miles. Between 0600 and 0800, Chazhma closed her position with the HGE to approximately two miles away.

At 1430, Chazhma closed to within one mile of the HGE. At 1540 there were Soviet personnel who began taking pictures from their boat deck using a binocular-type camera, and then their helicopter was launched and made many approaches to the HGE for approximately the next hour taking photographs from all angles. The Mission Director, with crates already stacked on the helicopter deck, sent a number of crew members to the bow of the HGE to preclude any attempt by the Soviet helicopter to hover and lower personnel there. At 1619, to the relief of the HGE, their helicopter landed back aboard Chazhma. Although the Mission Director and his team found it difficult to assess any Soviet intentions with the many close passes and scrutiny given to the HGE by the helicopter, the consensus was it ranged from being a thorough photographic assignment, to becoming a downright aggressive and provocative act.

These actions by Chazhma caused a measure of concern that the Soviets had become knowledgeable from other sources of the true mission of the HGE. After all, the HGE was vulnerable while sitting alone out in the vast Pacific Ocean—miles away from any friendly supporting forces—and very much aware of other unidentified contacts in the vicinity, which the communications unit had picked up on during the preceding few days. Accordingly, the Mission Director advised the officer in charge to be prepared to order emergency destruction of sensitive material which could compromise the mission if the Soviets attempted to board the ship. Team members designated to defend the control room (long enough to destroy important material) were alerted, but guns weren't issued.

At 1630, Chazhma started blinking a light signal to the HGE which was difficult to read because of the lighting conditions. The Soviet ship then passed 500 yards astern of the HGE and signaled they would communicate using the local code. The HGE responded with its own signal flag signifying "I am going to communicate with your station by means of international code signals." The HGE's communication unit then received an indication that another Soviet helicopter launch was pending. A few minutes later, Chazhma put up a flag hoist signifying "Understand your signal," then crossed the bow of the HGE at a distance of 1,000 yards. During all this surveillance the HGE remained stationary in the water. At 1711 hours, Chazhma transmitted by radio in Russian requesting acknowledgement if their transmission was heard. The HGE didn't answer back. At approximately 1730, Chazhma's helicopter took off and again made many low passes over the Glomar Explorer taking pictures of the ship. About one-half hour later, the helicopter completed its work and landed back aboard the Chazhma.

After several hours of attempts to respond to communications from the Soviet ship, Chazhma transmitted at 1847 "WCHG (HGE) this is UMGT" and indicated that they were ready for the HGE's message. The HGE answered "We have no message—but understand you have a message for us." The Soviet ship replied "Stand by five minutes" and then shortly afterwards transmitted "We are on our way home and heard your fog horn. What are you doing here?" This statement appeared questionable since Chazhma wasn't within hearing range during the fog. In any case, the HGE answered "We are conducting ocean mining tests—deep-ocean mining tests." Chazhma asked "What kind of vessel are you?" to which the HGE replied "A deep-ocean mining vessel." The Soviets then wanted to know what kind of equipment was aboard the HGE, to which the answer was "We have experimental deep-ocean mining equipment aboard." The Soviets asked "How much time will you be here?" and the HGE answered "We expect to finish testing in two to three weeks." The Soviet ship signed off with "I wish you all the best." Chazhma left the recovery area at about 2100 hours on the 18th of July and sailed off headed to Petropavlovsk.

Soviet Surveillance:

*I*t *is interesting to note the differences between sides on how this ship came to arrive. Apparently the Soviet* command had been suspicious of the Glomar Explorer having arrived near the larger search area for the lost submarine. This strange ship was reported and determined to be acting in a manner that suggested she could be involved in search operations. So the Soviet High Command wanted to send a couple of ships out to investigate her. However due to their own schedule, there were no ships available on a moments notice to be crewed and sent out to the area. The Soviet Navy at that time was being run on a very tight budget, and no nearby ships were available.

But by chance there were ships being used south of the Hawaiian Islands near Skwajanami Atoll, this was to support the flight of cosmonauts as directed by the Moscow Space Center. And one ship, the Chazhma, was scheduled to leave the area and head north, so a coded message was relayed to stop at the coordinates of the Glomar Explorer, and investigate. Orders were to pay particular attention to the type of activity underway and any possible recovery operations.

The Chazhma eventually arrived at the location days later, and the Commander aboard relayed an incredible scene of what they saw: a ship much larger than a soccer field with platforms and a huge lift system began using strange devices to lift metal pipes and then lower them underwater. Like clockwork they were attaching more long pipes by screwing these together, then sending them underwater and moving on to add even more pieces. Pipe by pipe this went on, as the Chazhma crew all watched it happening while in disbelief.

The Soviet command asked for them to determine if it's possible they could be using such a system to raise the lost submarine. The quick answer came back—it doesn't seem possible. The ship must be looking for oil or drilling for other resources. The next order was for the Chazhma to leave the area and return to port, since her food stores were nearly depleted.

AZORIAN Mission, 18 July—31 July 1974:

Fortunately the visibility cleared substantially on the 19th of July, and on the 20th of July all systems were still performing at operating conditions, but surging was still a particular concern due to a five-foot heaving of the HGE. On the morning of the 22nd, a 155-foot Soviet seagoing salvage tug, the SB-10, suddenly arrived and maintained a distance of about 3 to 4 miles. Work aboard the HGE continued, however.

The Soviet SB-10 then began a closer surveillance, passing to within 200 feet and making runs up and down both sides of the Glomar Explorer. HGE personnel observed (over time) 43 crew members (including one woman) on deck aboard the SB-10. They were dressed in fatigue-type outfits, swim trunks, shorts, and other such apparel. About a half-dozen Soviet sailors with cameras took photographs of the Glomar Explorer. By 2300 hours, the SB-10 had moved off to a distance of several miles again.

The HGE continued lowering pipe on the 24th of July and, despite more problems, the work aboard ship continued. Also the Pcllcas, a Greek ship, passed within two miles of the HGE without incident. Meanwhile, the SB-10 began another close surveillance of the HGE, frequently passing at short distances.

The HGE kept headquarters informed of engineering problems they was encountering. For example, it was reported on the 25th of July that malfunctions of the recovery system continued to make the situation difficult, but not discouraging. It was indicated that frequent shutdowns were experienced, mostly associated with the heavy-lift sensors and controls.

During the mission at this time one of the more repetitive jobs became the routine destruction of any classified documents aboard. An early solution to this problem was to hand-tear small amounts of paper into tiny pieces and dump them over the side. One night while the paper was being dumped, the old axiom "don't spit into the wind" was relearned at the cost of anxious moments being spent gathering up tiny pieces of paper from the main deck. More unclassified paper trash (mostly old invoices) dumped overboard by the Global Marine supply man ended up being promptly collected by the inquisitive Soviet crew during surveillance. Thanks to these lessons, the security officer aboard the Glomar Explorer began using a paper shredder which turned all classified paper into a powder-like material for dumping overboard at night.

Finally on the 26th of July, the Command-Control Van reported sonar contact with the ocean bottom. By this time, the series of equipment breakdowns which had occurred were beginning to wear on the nerves of the recovery team. A bright side to all these problems, however, was the confidence the crew began to have in the pipe, which seemed able to bounce back from nearly all kinds of abuse and remain unscarred. On this date, the Mission Director reported that 230 doubles, or 13,800 feet of pipe, had now been deployed. Meanwhile, the nearby SB-10 continued their surveillance.

On the 28th of July, a major piece of equipment failed, causing a display of noise with sparks and smoke, including a spastic shaking of the derrick. These effects were startling, to say the least, but no insurmountable damage was suffered. It was reported that many among the crew became nervous about the safety of the heavy-lift system and, as a precaution, unneeded personnel were now kept away from the work area around the A-frame.

While this situation was being corrected, high resolution sonars were being used to pinpoint the target submarine. Meanwhile, the SB-10 stayed within radar range at approximately 5 miles while a heavy fog prevailed, limiting visibility to less than one mile.

An HGE crew member recalls the excitement from here: "Suddenly everyone onboard was caught up in the anticipation of seeing the target object for the first time. The main source of action was the control center. All eyes were watching the display from the scanning sonars (our long-range detectors) for any sign of a return. The yellow dots marched across the cathode ray tube in unending regularity. Then, on one pass, an irregular hemispherical hump displaced the flat line on the screen. One, two, three, ... and more times it was the same. It was the submarine hulk for sure. Word spread rapidly throughout the ship. We were on target!"

"Within hours we were close enough to the target for the TV cameras to pick up a clear picture of the remains of the submarine. All hands wanted to see the picture, and the Mission Director allowed the crew, in small groups, to file through the control center to see it for themselves."

"The Mission Director and his deputies recognized that during actual recovery operations the ship's crew couldn't be allowed in the control center. The concentration and tension would be too great to risk any distractions. The crew had contributed greatly to the project's success, and denying them a chance to observe the recovery operation weighed heavily on the Mission Director's mind. So he directed that several TV monitors be placed around the ship for the crew's benefit to see the video. These were intently watched by the sailors, cooks, divers, and drill crew—all hands—during the crucial moments of the recovery."

There was one last hiccup from the pipe-handling system that night. As a 15-ton pipe double was being placed in the cart, it slipped over the center joint stop used to restrain the pipe and became loose in the cart. The galley and port-deck sleeping areas near the transfer boom were evacuated until the pipe was back under control. Once again, fortunately, no personnel injury or damage to the system resulted from the accident.

Meanwhile, the SB-10 maintained its usual surveillance activity of closing in towards the HGE and then drifting off for a couple of miles. Generally, the visibility remained poor, at less than two miles, and the HGE sounded her fog signal during these low-visibility conditions. The next string, pipe No. 268 was put into the upper yoke, but at this stage the pipe was moving very slowly, with only a few more necessary to reach the bottom.

The Deputy for Recovery reported the following information to headquarters: "the heavy lift system is operating marginally; two additional heave compensator position transmitters failed; the target was easily located...high resolution sonar and video are excellent; and the salt water (seawater) hydraulic flow to test the hydraulic system was checked out...preparations are continuing...one heave compensator position transmitter was repaired."

The SB-10 tug still remained within close range during the night, and was illuminated with a searchlight from the HGE whenever it maneuvered uncomfortably close. This tactic was always successful in making the SB-10 move off. It continued its close-in surveillance of the HGE in the morning, then circled the ship once, and was observed taking height and distance measurements of the HGE's substructure using a sextant and an alidade.

On the 31st of July, Headquarters was informed that some problems had been experienced overnight but the heave compensator position indicators were working well and all systems were normal. Optics remained good while mud at the ocean bottom had obscured visibility for about one-half hour.

Soviet Retaliation:

*I*n *July the safe of Howard Hughes was burglarized for documents relating to this mission. Who and how this came to be wasn't said, but it was assumed a million dollars was offered for this information. Somehow this information was* retrieved and eventually made its way to the U.S. press and into newspapers. The Glomar Explorer was said to be an invention years ahead of its time, which also allowed for the recreation of this entire episode, with a code name of Operation JENNIFER.

When copies of these documents eventually got back to the Soviet Main HQ, they were in amazement that such a thing could be carried out. Fleet HQ had their phones ringing and answers were demanded. How could such an operation be attempted? Yelling and cursing followed. An entire explanation was demanded in only two hours!

Lift-off:

On the 1st of August, the submarine began to be lifted from the bottom, and by 2200 that night, the recovery was well underway. During all this time, the SB-10 appeared to be running in circles, moving in at close distances to all points of the ship. In addition, other unidentified radar contacts were reported within a short range of the ship as well. Pipe lifting went well on the 2nd of August and the weather cooperated.

Meanwhile, the Mission Director instructed his team to start preparations for entrance into Midway in accordance with the AZORIAN operations and cover plans. In total, two hundred and seventy-four doubles or 16,440 feet of pipe had been deployed and were coming up in progress. (Figures 35 and 36.)

In accordance with the cover plan, a message went out using an open commercial channel on the 3rd of August to explain entry into Midway. The Glomar Explorer duly reported that it believed the "nodule collector vehicle" had collided with a hard silt-covered outcrop. It was this fictional "casualty," reported out in the clear, which was used as an excuse for the HGE to request permission from the U.S. Naval authorities to enter Midway for repairs to the vehicle.

This scenario would follow that the damage to the "nodule collector" was more serious than at first diagnosed, and a new part would be required from the U.S. mainland for repairs.

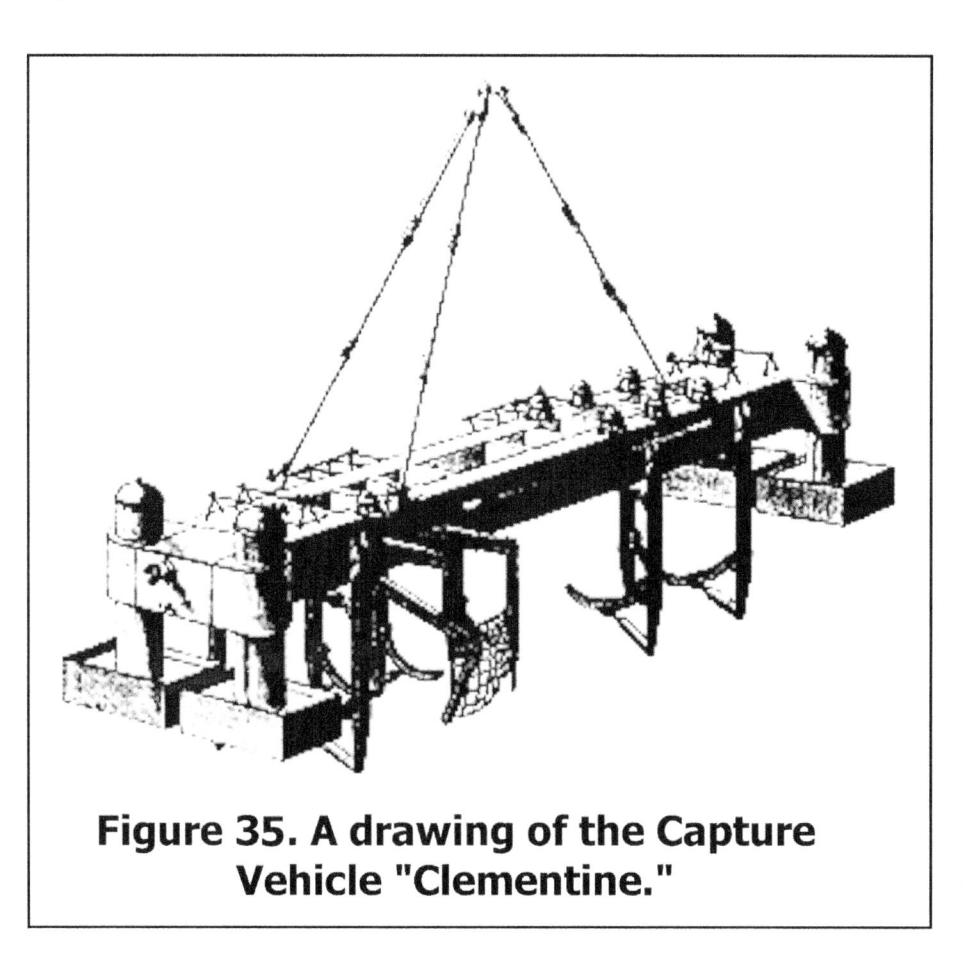

Figure 35. A drawing of the Capture Vehicle "Clementine."

In contrast, a factual coded message was also sent out that same day pointing out how the operation was still plagued with serious heavy-lift problems, even as the load on the pipe was decreasing. At high pressures, the heavy-lift hydraulic pumps required much attention, and a great deal of trouble was experienced in keeping a sufficient number of them operable. Because of these conditions, it was necessary to bypass some fail-safe circuitry and depend instead on operating personnel.

Figure 36. Positioning and lifting "Clementine" for the recovery.

The operators and hydraulic mechanics were complimented for doing what the Mission Director judged was an outstanding job, and he expressed pleasure that the ship had overcome some major hurdles while facing up to all the problems associated with the recovery operations.

Unfortunately during the lift when the submarine was a third of the way up, she broke apart, and a large section plunged back to the ocean bottom. Crestfallen, the Glomar Explorer crew continued hauling up the portion that remained in the capture vehicle. All hands were very busy and concerned, knowing the many times they came close to aborting the mission because of equipment problems. The mission team wasn't discouraged into quitting, however, and had every intention of accomplishing the objective of raising the remaining part of the submarine to the surface.

Meanwhile, the SB-10 continued its close surveillance nearby. During the preceding night, the tanker Bangkok (Thailand registry) had passed by within five miles of the Glomar Explorer. A short series of flashing light exchanges passed between the Bangkok and the HGE, and there was also an exchange via radio. The Bangkok asked questions as to the operations being conducted, and the HGE replied briefly that she was conducting experimental deep-ocean mining operations. The query from the Bangkok appeared to stem from curiosity and was judged to be purely social in nature. It was also concluded that the SB-10's presence near the recovery site was related to a Soviet Pacific Fleet submarine operation and transit.

Still, the HGE team maintained their composure and adhered to the AZORIAN cover plan by sending a commercial message via station KPH in San Francisco advising that the "nodule collector vehicle" might be more damaged than originally thought.

On the 6th of August, the HGE received a message from Paul Reeve, the Summa Ocean Mining Division General Manager, addressed to "the Senior Summa Representative" aboard the ship. This overt commercial message instructed that as soon as the Summa representative was in a position to assess the damage to the "nodule collector vehicle," he was to start reporting at least twice daily on their progress towards going about getting effective repairs.

Meanwhile, the SB-10 continued to operate in close range as the submarine portion was raised closer to the well of the HGE. On the afternoon of the 5th of August, the HGE executed a plan to lower the docking legs to 90 feet, tilt them in and out, and then move them slowly back to their previous position. This drill attempted to elicit any possible reaction that the SB-10 might be planning to take.

Although the SB-10 started to close its distance with the HGE when it saw the docking legs being lowered, its maneuvers generally were no different from what it had previously conducted.

On the 6th of August, the SB-10 again maneuvered completely around the HGE, closing to within a distance of only 75 yards. The Glomar Explorer gave a flashing light signal to warn the SB-10 to keep clear because the ship was "maneuvering with difficulty."

Ironically, the SB-10's capabilities as a vessel were considered to include a limited shallow-water diver ability normally used to support submarine contingency situations and minor salvage roles. This capability indicated that both hard-hat and Scuba divers were trained to perform hull inspection and repairs under controlled conditions at depths of less than 30 feet. However, headquarters didn't believe the Soviet tug personnel would have the training or experience to accomplish this dangerous task of underwater reconnaissance of the HGE. The divers could easily be observed, and the risk of injury or death in open ocean near an unknown objective would be so great as to not be acceptable. The Mission Director and his advisors had in any case devised a few simple ship maneuvers to counter possible Soviet divers without endangering the mission.

As work progressed onboard, the lifting operation had now become more comfortable. Pressure in the hydraulic power units was dropping and had fallen to almost a routine level. Each double of pipe removed meant about 15 tons less load on the system. No one was relaxing, but there was a sense arising that they were actually going to make it.

AT 2135, the SB-10 again approached the HGE to within 75 yards on her starboard beam. The HGE sent a warning signal to the SB-10 to keep clear. The Soviet tug backed off, sounded three long blasts of her whistle and went around the stern of the HGE while still at a distance of about 75 yards. Then the SB-10 crew members were observed waving. The tug appeared to be headed home for Petropavlovsk, and by 2238 it was fading from the HGE's radar screen. Its departure marked the end of a close surveillance of the HGE which had lasted for 13 days and 16 hours.

A touch of irony was that as the SB-10 had broken off its close-in surveillance, the recovered K-129 submarine was right below the HGE. One can only conjecture the reaction and chagrin of Soviet authorities when they later realized that two Soviet Navy vessels were on scene and, in effect, had witnessed the recovery operation against their lost submarine.

Later that day, the Mission Director reported on problems the recovery team still encountered. For example, the heavy-lift system had a leaking seal on the upper yoke, and sticking isolation valves were making the system dangerous; three hydraulic pumps had blown manifolds, and difficulty was being experienced keeping them running at the proper pressure. Other problems occurred and were corrected as quickly as possible so that the recovery could proceed. All this was transmitted as a matter of routine in a status report on engineering matters—rather than an emotional litany of calamities, as might have occurred in such a stressful situation. No radioactive contamination had been detected as yet.

An HGE crew member recalls from there: "Finally the Soviet tug had left. We were going to be able to do the telltale pump-down operations without surveillance. Our cover story had held: the Soviets had been fooled. Now we could anticipate seeing our prize without being concerned about sharing it with the owner."

"Everyone wanted to get a first glimpse of the target. Those of us waiting anxiously on deck received a reward of a different type. Bobbing up to the surface (luckily in the well) was a brimming full Jerry-can of torpedo juice. It had traveled over three miles to the bottom and back and been subjected to pressures of over 7000 pounds per square inch without spilling a drop."

"The Mission Director and his team viewed this scene from a balcony-like portion of the ladder which led down to the well-gates. Radiation monitors had reported readings 5 times background even at this distance. We knew that we were in for a nasty time. Some of the earlier excitement of the mission was returning to the exploitation party. It was going to be difficult—the jumbled hulk wasn't going to reveal its secrets easily."

Then while the water was being pumped out and before shoring began, an inspection team checked the target for nuclear contamination. More evidence of plutonium was found. As the inspection and exploitation continued, the contamination was found to be coming primarily from one or more of the nuclear torpedoes whose high explosives had detonated without creating a nuclear explosion—the war heads were "one point safe." Fortunately, the plutonium was in a hydroxide form and thus there was little danger for any airborne particulate.

Soviet Surveillance:

*A**nother nearby vessel, the rescue tug SB-10 became available before the Chazhma had departed the area and was sent to the area by Fleet Command. This wasn't nearly the impressive ship, being only a tug that had a civilian captain, and while they tried their best when observing things, there wasn't much left to report. And when the food stores aboard were nearly gone, off to port the tug was ordered.*

Afterwards we instead started to send long-range reconnaissance aircraft over the area, but not much information could be determined from such a high altitude.

Only to confirm the location of the ship, and at what time. Only a few trips were possible.

Then something interesting happened, we noticed a change in communications. The ship started sending messages through secure channels, and they determined the ship must be involved in the lost submarine. Urgently it was decided to send another naval ship to the area.

After much paper shuffling, it ended up being acted upon, but this turned out to be too late. Theories on why the United Sates would raise the sub were offered, with one suggesting the U.S. was desperate to break the radio codes from shore to submarine. But with such outdated information aboard, it was determined to be of no practical importance even if lost. While the deep-sea bathyscaphe Trieste II had earlier mapped this area of the Pacific, with additional information it was still doubtful they'd be able to raise everything.

Also of note it was determined a sinking of the submarine alone and loss at depth wasn't enough to give an accurate location, but only a collision could offer enough precision to allow an accurate search, at least in theory. And it was known that a ship called the Glomar Challenger had earlier visited the area, but for what reason, the Soviet HQ were unsure. It was assumed to give cover as though she was doing the survey work, when it was really the Trieste II.

Another code expert suggested a better reason: they wanted the outdated codes to help develop ciphers to break current codes being used, and as such they would be extremely valuable. Also to acquire the technology systems with weapons, training books, and manuals aboard.

The Glomar Explorer was known to have been built with pieces coming from separate shipyards. Those actually doing the construction work couldn't guess the eventual use of such a vessel. The important part beyond the structure was a state of the art station keeping system that used 4 thrusters and satellite guidance to maintain her stationary over an object at sea to within a single foot. Threaded pipes were lowered through a well, or moon pool, and were connected to the main recovery apparatus which included observation equipment. Another vessel was used for the actual docking and recovery, using a giant claw that was formed in the shape of the Soviet submarine. It included stoppers for attachment and would squeeze around the hull itself, prior to raising.

Clementine was the nickname given to the large submersible claw that the Glomar Explorer lowered to the bottom of the ocean. The lowering to the depths went well, but with only about 50 feet left or so to go, the operator got overanxious and struck the submarine with too much force (distances underwater are difficult to measure due to refraction and visibility). One claw on Clementine barely cracked on impact, but, after an adjustment, it was able to clamp onto the submarine correctly. Then they began raising it slowly.

After it came a ways up, the fractured claw with two others broke away, leaving insufficient claws remaining to maintain the total weight. Then as the unseen crack amidships widened before anyone could do anything, the entire aft end began falling away. Only the forward portion was able to be brought into the Glomar Explorer, which consisted of the forward two compartments (having the radio room and an old code room), along with two nuclear torpedoes. This section was taken inside of the moon pool, and secured as a prize. Once this area was pumped dry, the opening team went in to assess what they had.

Recovery Completed:

The recovery phase of the AZORIAN mission was finished on the 9th of August. In a commercial message sent to "Summa headquarters" via Station KPH, San Francisco, the HGE advised she had completed "Event 36-A," a prearranged code for the recovery phase. Previously, other major events had been coded sequentially to keep headquarters informed about the mission's progress. In accordance with the AZORIAN cover plan, mention was also made that a damage analysis of the "nodule collector vehicle" was still progressing.

Despite a certain amount of apprehension due to past and a potential future presence of Soviet ships at the recovery site, it was decided that all residual actions, such as recovery of the wave rider buoys, should still be completed. After all, the buoys total cost was about $25,000, and it was pointed out that the situation wouldn't improve appreciably by scurrying away from the site before completing everything that needed be done. If the Soviet Navy were inclined to challenge the HGE, the ship couldn't outrun them. Thus, the HGE continued carrying out her cover role as a commercial mining research ship according to plan.

The HGE sent a commercial message on the 10th of August, ostensibly to Summa, stating that every effort was being made to determine whether a repair of the nodule collector vehicle could be made at sea. At that time, the ship was continuing her course towards a prearranged site in the direction of Midway Island where, under the cover plan, a decision would be made as to whether it was necessary to enter Midway.

On the 11th of August, the HGE sent another commercial message indicating she was changing her destination to a new site and that repairs to the "nodule collector vehicle" would take at least 30 days to complete. A decision had been made by headquarters that the ship should proceed to Lahaina Roads off the Island of Maui in the Hawaiian Islands, where a crew change would be made. A special exploitation team to recover, process, and package the recovered intelligence items also would board the ship in Hawaii.

The HGE sent another commercial message on the 12th of August for cover reasons stating that the "nodule collector vehicle" would be ready for inspection and commencement of the repair work upon arrival at Site 130-1, which was Lahaina Roads. Arrangements were made for an inspection team from Washington to examine what was recovered. For cover purposes, Paul Reeve, General Manager, Summa Ocean Mining Division, would lead this team aboard the ship.

Meanwhile, a series of personal messages were sent from crew members not under cover to make arrangements for relatives and friends to meet them either in Honolulu or on the West Coast.

The HGE arrived and anchored at Lahaina Roads at 1430 local time, on the 16th of August. The mission crew was relieved by the exploitation crew in the evening, and Paul Reeve and the engineering inspection group boarded the HGE at that time. In Hawaii, the Honolulu Advertiser newspaper featured a front page article about the HGE and the Summa mining venture. On the 17th of August, the Summa office at Honolulu maintained its cover image by sending a message via RCA, San Francisco to its home office advising that the crew change had gone smoothly. The HGE was initially anchored approximately one mile south of the Lahaina Roads sea buoy, but later that morning she shifted anchorage to a point eight miles south of Lahaina Roads buoy, approximately five miles offshore.

Condition Of The Submarine:

The Glomar Explorer had left and headed to the Hawaiian Islands, where in shallow waters, those portions of the submarine left were lowered to the bottom so divers could inspect them more closely and recover what remained, including important documents.

To the amazement of everyone, the great ocean pressures at those depths encountered had made things twist and shrink to sizes much smaller than was imaginable—items like mattresses in the sleeping area had shrunk to the size of a paperback book. They also recovered six Soviet bodies from inside the sub, with those being in the forward areas. It was postulated that the locations weren't consistent with a general emergency, but rather were in areas such as while watching a movie or generally relaxing while under snorkel. This is why the loss must have been sudden, they all died in almost a peaceful state. Only one officer was among those recovered. Once this recovery was completed, all submariners were given a proper burial at sea with the playing of the Soviet Anthem, after which they were lowered together in a single large casket.

Among the documents retrieved wasn't what the U.S. had hoped for. While the missiles system was found, the code room wasn't where it should've been. Apparently the tall Captain had requested it be moved farther aft so he wouldn't hit his head on the tiny entryways.

Everything that became known about the recovery was sent to Moscow, where they studied things for two days. The Soviet Ministry of Foreign Affairs eventually sent a note to the United States: "Your country raised our sunken submarine in violation of international law." The U.S. State Department replied: "You failed to report the loss of your submarine, so the rules of international law don't apply here." A second note was sent: "But you retrieved the bodies of our lost submariners, and permanently invaded their gravesite." The note back replied: "Not at all, they were buried at sea according to your Soviet customs, and a copy of the recorded movie is being sent."

Yet nothing could be done, the recovery had already taken place. Moscow could only posture and put a ship in the area of the loss to prevent any further efforts.

Meanwhile, some at Fleet HQ still questioned if the recovery had even happened.

On a side note about the successful raising, the CIA had planned to go back and try to recovered the remaining portions that had broken away. However a leak to the newspapers in America had brought this to the attention of Capital Hill in Washington, where senators demanded to know all about the project, including the costs involved and how it was authorized. That attention pretty much killed off any chance of returning to the site to finish a recovery.

For years later our government barely recognized the loss of the submarine within our own country. Families weren't told about how their loved ones had died, and were only given death certificates that stated—Declared Dead. There was no explanation given, no location shown, no reasons stated. Families could only rely on rumors about the loss at sea and when it had sunk. There wasn't even an official list of those missing being published anywhere.

The loss of the submarine probably happened when she turned onto a new heading, one not noted by the sub following her, the USS *Swordfish*. An under portion below the control room was unintentionally struck and caused the central area to be flooded on impact.

But why try a recovery for this target, and not the later model Soviet submarine K-8, which had sunk in April of 1970 about 300 miles NW of Spain? She went down in shallower waters and also went unreported as to location. She even used nuclear propulsion, and perhaps that's why they left her alone, when K-129 only had nuclear warheads to worry about. (Also at the time of the loss of K-129, the earlier special ammunition designs were no longer in production and weren't being adapted to newer designs.) After the loss, all Fleet documents and ciphers were changed accordingly.

Mission Analysis:

Looking back on the AZORIAN operation, the Mission Director remarked that he was extremely grateful for the advice and confidence he received from William Colby, Director of Central Intelligence, immediately prior to the HGE's departure for the AZORIAN mission in June. Colby told him he was fully aware of what it meant to operate in the field, and that the officer-in-charge at the scene of action is usually much more aware of a given situation than someone back at headquarters. Therefore, Colby said he wanted to assure the Mission Director that he was to use his own good judgment in critical situations as long as he was adhering to the basic guidelines of the directives and plans which governed the operation. In looking back to that challenging and very difficult experience, the Mission Director recounted that he took this advice gratefully and literally.

Thus, the long saga of AZORIAN came to a conclusion as the HGE rested at anchor in the Hawaiian Islands, more than six years since the Soviet G-II-class submarine K-129 sank in the Northwest Pacific Ocean. The efforts to locate the site of the sinking and to conceive, develop, build, and deploy the HGE recovery system stretched almost as long in time, beginning in mid-1968. And the success that was achieved depended, in the end, on the combined skills of a multitude of people in government and industry who together forged the capability that made it possible to proceed with such an incredible project. And as the operational phase of AZORIAN ended, the important task of exploiting the intelligence information began.

The news media leak to the Los Angeles Times in February of 1975, however, culminated in Jack Anderson's decision to expose the project on national TV and radio in March. As proof that the USSR had gotten the message—and no doubt it was intended as a message to us—the Soviets reacted immediately to the disclosure and assigned one of their ships to sit and monitor the site of their lost submarine, which had then become known to them.

One of the most difficult exercises is to apply the cost-benefit principle to a specific intelligence operation. This is particularly true with Project AZORIAN. During its early stages of planning, Deputy Secretary of Defense David Packard and his fellow ExCom members and other senior officials were wrestling with projected costs of the program and evaluating the technical risks involved. Lifting a submarine weighing approximately 1,750 tons from a depth of 16,500 feet had never been attempted or accomplished anywhere before. Packard contended if they were to wait until all the risks were eliminated, the project would never get started. The resulting decision to move ahead with the plan to recover the Soviet submarine was courageous, carefully considered, and intangibly beneficial: a government or organization too timid to undertake calculable risks in pursuit of a proper objective wouldn't be true to itself or to the people it serves. To attempt to evaluate Project AZORIAN in terms of cost benefits, one must consider not only the immediate intelligence gained, but the broader aspects and achievements as well. For example, the state-of-the-art in deep-ocean mining and heavy-lift technology was advanced in a major way. AZORIAN produced an advanced deep-ocean system with important future economic, political, and strategic potential for the United States. The need for such a capability is well-documented in the United Nations Law-of-the-Sea Negotiations. As a final note, this project was tangible proof that the intelligence profession is dynamic and alive—while keeping pace with the rapid advances within science and technology.

Soviet Legacy:

It took nearly 22 years for the Soviet Press to finally start reporting on the tragedy about the loss of K-129. And much of the reporting (in the sudden rush to be first) had conflicting information, such as differing dates on when the submarine left port, or how many persons were actually aboard. One claimed a United States satellite recorded a bright flash on the day of the accident, and even there were differing lengths to how long the sub went out on the mission (in particular, they even misspelled many crew member names, to the dismay of their family members).

Later reports in the U.S. Press theorized that the sub had surfaced to recharge her batteries, and perhaps a spark had lit off gasses within the hull. None of the crew were able to escape the disaster, and she sank to the bottom with all hands aboard. By chance a U.S. based system picked up the sound of the sub explosion, and set in motion a covert plan to eventually raise the sub to the surface. Meanwhile, our Soviet Union wasn't aware of this, or even of the area that the loss occurred. At the time we were mainly searching in a different area, which was probably to the delight of U.S. Intelligence.

But why wasn't the Soviet Press allowed to publish more during the time shortly after the recovery happened? Many believe that our Soviet government didn't want the facts to be known since Brezhnev was going to meet with President Ford, and they didn't want anti-American stories happening prior to those meetings. Some inside Moscow even felt as though the recovery was a technical marvel, something they wish we could accomplish, while still being upset with the handling of the Soviet seamen remains.

Comparisons were also made to the U-2 spy plane incident, which had occurred in 1960 after its pilot was captured. At that time a meeting was sabotaged between Khrushchev and President Eisenhower, when he openly admitted that they'd sent a spy plane over our country.

By contrast, this was a covert operation to raise something lost by another, but there was also the fact that we hadn't openly admitted to the sub being sunk in the first place. To protest too loudly might make this fact come back up within our own country, and was something better to be swept under the rug.

Even the U.S. Press articles had many variations on the facts of this project. From what was actually raised, to how many bodies were retrieved, to what sections were kept intact, to the circumstances on funding, on whether a safe was opened and documents stolen about the mission, etc. One enterprising article suggested that U.S. Intelligence would obtain all ciphers, codes, encrypted documents and machinery, nuclear technology, including submarine construction techniques. The $350 million cost to retrieve it all was worth that price, and more. With more bravado, they claimed a return trip to retrieve what was left behind was under planning, to be continued later.

Post-Mission Adjustments:

After the AZORIAN recovery operation in which three of the grabber arms failed, the CV design was re-examined in order to determine high stress points in the grabber arms. Four new beams and davits were fabricated from HY-100 steel and one from A-36 steel. This heavier but more forgiving steel could be used because the remaining target object was smaller, and its weight had been more accurately determined to be less than half the previously estimated weight. These facts dispelled the earlier concern that the heavy lift system would be stalled by an excessive load.

Since the breakout legs had been left at the target site, four new legs had to be fabricated for Clementine. The sonar and optic sensors were repositioned to match the new target configuration and pan/tilt controls were added to two TV cameras. All structures were given a thorough non-destructive inspection. After a successful systems test, Clementine was ready for a new attempt.

MATADOR Preparations:

After the decision was made to make a new attempt to complete the recovery mission, the Office of Security's thoughts turned towards the procedures to be used on the new program, code named MATADOR. A review of the procedures used on AZORIAN was necessary and carried out fully for preparations.

But in February of 1975 the Los Angeles Times combined four sure-fire headlines into one front-page story. It was about the unsolved Romaine Street robbery and Howard Hughes, the CIA, and the recovery of the sunken Soviet submarine. According to the Times, the CIA had attempted to recover the Soviet submarine from the depths of the ocean with a ship that Hughes had built with government money. The Times managed to link these rumors with a detailed recapitulation of the eight-month-old robbery of the Hughes office on Romaine Street in Encino, in which the burglars had made off with cash and "sensitive papers." Despite the obvious errors in this account, it unfortunately focused the attention of other journalists onto the Glomar Explorer.

For a while, DCI William Colby managed to hold the line against further revelations by personally appealing to the senior managers of the nation's news media, but in March Jack Anderson went on national television with his version, and the press floodgates were opened. MATADOR, however, wasn't yet wholly engulfed, and preparations continued for a mission start date in early July.

However, due to this exposure, the Glomar Explorer soon became a fortress besieged as local, regional and national news media poured into the Long Beach area. Helicopters carrying network television crews hovered over the ship. Reporters frequented the Long Beach bars and tried all the tricks of the trade into finding knowledgeable sources to get them to talk. Waterfront stragglers were plied with drinks, and prostitutes were enlisted in attempts to buy crew lists.

Crew members were pestered, badgered and propositioned. The security team gave repeated crew briefings into the dangers of having conversations with people from the news media; their admonition was: "Don't answer any questions, no matter how trivial about the Glomar Explorer or her purpose." The crew and other workers within the program responded by holding the line, even when the press got after their families at home or came at them directly with offers for substantial sums of money.

Only one internal breach marred the record, and security quickly tracked it down. A story appearing in the New York Times in early April of 1975—though it contained much that was wrong and was designed to be provocative—it revealed information that must have been obtained only from an insider. Clues within the story pointed in one direction, particularly a reference to the issuing of boots to a new crew member. The logistics records were searched, the receipt for the boots was found, and the leaker got uncovered. He was an office worker who'd been with the program for only four months during 1974, resigning shortly before he would've been dismissed. He hadn't worked aboard the ship, but had a younger brother among the "B" crew, the one that had met the ship in Hawaii to relieve the recovery crew. While under the influence of his older brother, this crew member had discussed aspects of the mission, but it was the older brother who went to the New York Times with his own cockeyed, contentious version. Security couldn't do anything at the time except redouble their warnings to the crew members and everyone else connected with the program to maintain the "no comment" policy.

Another incident occurred as the ship was being readied for the new attempt. The Long Beach Harbor Patrol had official access to the pier, and on one occasion a uniformed Harbor Patrol officer accompanied by a civilian drove to the gangway leading up to the main deck of the ship. The civilian jumped out and began taking pictures—a strictly forbidden activity—and then quickly drove away. Security, through the Global Marine superintendent, phoned the Harbor Patrol and explained what had happened. The Harbor Patrol authorities, chagrined, investigated and found the officer responsible for the intrusion. The film was returned undeveloped with an apology. The guilty officer claimed he was only helping a college friend do a story on the types of ships within the Long Beach Harbor.

Security measures on the ship were increased in reaction not only to all these happenings, but to a wave of bomb threats in the general Los Angeles area. The concern for security was reinforced after a Catalina tour boat was targeted and destroyed by a radical group at a pier in the nearby Los Angeles Harbor. Howard Hughes and his reported relationship with CIA made the Glomar Explorer a natural target for the radicals, and security mounted a deck watch to warn of any suspicious approaches to the ship from the harbor channel.

Anti-swimming nets were made and kept handy on the main deck to be used against any swimmers approaching the ship. The guard force at the pier gate was increased, and any packages, sacks or bags going on the pier had to be opened, inspected, and stamped by security. No explosives were going to go on the ship through deliberate attempts or by the duping of innocents.

Vigilance against Soviet observation and espionage was also maintained. Russian ships were constantly docking at a pier directly across the channel, while precious little shipping activity seemed to be taking place around them. The opening of hatches which exposed the well area to photographic surveillance had to get the approval of the security officer. Yet no overt or covert interest in the Glomar Explorer by the Russian ships was ever observed.

Phase-out:

Everything remained busy as the crew was putting the ship through her paces, until in late June when word came down that the MATADOR mission was canceled. There would only be one last trip to sea for the Glomar Explorer and her crew, and that would be for the purpose of a final clean-up. Then a few days prior to departure, the tax assessor of Los Angeles County slapped a tax lien on the ship for $4,685,882.07 and seized the vessel, and was going to put her up for sale at a public auction to be held on the 27th of August, 1975. The assessor sent a watch keeper to the pier to prevent the ship from departing. While he was watching the ship, the onboard security officer was watching him. The eyeball-to-eyeball confrontation was resolved within days by the necessary legal maneuvers. The Glomar Explorer departed the pier on the 20th of August for her final clean-up.

Meanwhile, although the government maintained its "no comment" stance after the Jack Anderson expose in March, all the newspapers continued to trumpet the story—playing and replaying articles combining the wildest of speculation, invention, half-truths, conjecture and fragments of the facts. In this they inadvertently served the security interests of the government, for it looked very much as if the Soviets were as confused about the mission's purpose and degree of success as were ordinary American readers. It was security's job to keep it that way; there was to be no confirmation or denial of any of the stories circulating in the press.

This became a delicate task as the program phase-out began. Crew members and other workers were laid off, since only a small maintenance force was to be kept aboard the ship. The debriefings by security had to be done in a way that would minimize the chances that employees would leave the program with a grudge against it; news stories could easily result from such sources. The debriefings were conducted professionally and with empathy towards the work force. No leaks to the press resulted from the crew roll-off procedures.

A serious effort was made to find alternate uses for the ship; the General Services Administration undertook this responsibility along with Global Marine, Inc. When tours of the ship were arranged for interested parties, it was security's job to make sure the critical spaces were avoided. The control center was the only major portion that needed protecting.

Global Marine was permitted to make a commercial movie about the Glomar Explorer in order to advertise her capabilities. Richard Anderson from the Six Million Dollar Man television series was the narrator. Again some glamour returned to the ship, and again security had to be alert to prevent any would-be movie stars among the crew from making unauthorized film debuts. Also, certain areas of the ship had to remain protected from the camera's sweeping eye.

Then in November of 1975 the government's onboard security officer was removed and replaced by a former employee hired on contract. By now the ship was in a configuration in which there was essentially no chance for erosion of security.

Efforts to find alternate uses for the ship hadn't been successful, and there was little activity onboard other than routine maintenance. Finally, when the U.S. Navy took over control of the Glomar Explorer and started the mothballing process, a staff security officer returned to the ship during the turnover activities to conduct a physical inspection in conjunction with officers from the Navy and the Maritime Administration.

After a couple of years in mothballs, the Glomar Explorer was reactivated for legitimate deep-ocean mining tests. While the ship was in drydock for refurbishment, some material was found in a remote part of the well that looked suspiciously like remnants of Soviet canned goods, either cabbage or carrots, left over from the exploitation of the submarine. The item was quickly and carefully sequestered by some of the ship's crew who had remembered their lectures on security and radioactive contamination. A team of experts was sent to examine the find. It turned out to be non-radioactive sauerkraut of U.S. origin.

However the Glomar's brief career was now over, and after some experimental ocean mining voyages sponsored by a consortium of industry leaders, she was mothballed at anchor for over a quarter century as part of the Suisun Bay Reserve Fleet in California. Then in the late 1990's, a U.S. petroleum company restored the ship for use in deep-sea oil drilling and exploration. Renamed the GSF Explorer, the ship was still being used for that purpose until June of 2015, when she sadly was sent off to China for scrapping due to a slump in oil prices.

Although Project AZORIAN failed to meet its full intelligence objectives, the CIA considers it to be one of the greatest intelligence coups of the Cold War. Project AZORIAN remains an engineering marvel through its state of the art advancement in deep-ocean mining and heavy-lift technology.

Valediction:

It's been said that a program designed to have no risk has the best security. Too often this implies no action and no results. AZORIAN was a high-risk program, full of action and results. The security afforded to it was the best available.

A Final Word:

The equipment developed for Project AZORIAN continued on living. After a period in mothballs, the HGE was eventually reactivated as an honest-to-goodness mining ship. A consortium led by Lockheed used the ship and the pipe string to test a mining machine. The world's largest submersible (HMB-1) was used by the Department of Energy in their ocean thermal energy conversion program. The San Francisco Bay base for the HMB-1 was used by the U.S. Coast and Geodetic Survey as an operational location. The Nuclear Regulatory Commission once made inquiries about the proof test machine to test steel plates. Even a part of Clementine (the CV) found a use. One of her arms was part of a tensile test facility in Southern California. And the same technology developed for the AZORIAN simulator was used to train operators to emplace a huge offshore oil platform. That platform, costing $750 million, was constructed in several hundred feet of water off the Louisiana Coast. In this way the training procedures and hardware developed for AZORIAN played a further role in helping to develop the oil resources of the United States.

So the labor of love created by a group of Agency managers and engineers has borne a continuing reward, and although the Glomar Explorer no longer sails on the high seas, she was an amazing ship that kept her secrets well.

The End

Printed in Great Britain
by Amazon